THE NEW IMMIGRANTS

The New Immigrants

CAROL OLSEN DAY
EDMUND DAY

A GROLIER COMPANY

Franklin Watts
New York/London/Toronto/Sydney/1985
An Impact Book

Library of Congress Cataloging in Publication Data

Day, Carol Olsen.
The new immigrants.

(An Impact book)
Bibliography: p.
Includes index.
Summary: Describes the present condition of both legal and illegal immigration in the United States. Also discusses the problems and controversies connected with present-day immigrants and the changes that are needed in the immigration laws.
1. United States—Emigration and immigration—Juvenile literature. 2. United States—Emigration and immigration—Government policy—Juvenile literature. [1. United States—Emigration and immigration] I. Day, Edmund. II. Title.
JV6455.D32 1985 325.73 84-25761
ISBN 0-531-04929-9

Printed in the United States of America
5 4 3 2 1

CONTENTS

1 *Chapter One*
Our Teeming Shores

13 *Chapter Two*
Legal Immigrants:
Hispanics and Asians

27 *Chapter Three*
Bilingualism and Upward Mobility

35 *Chapter Four*
Refugees:
Indochinese Exodus

49 *Chapter Five*
Refugees:
Settling in the United States

57 *Chapter Six*
Refugees:
Cubans, Central Americans, Haitians, and Soviets

75 *Chapter Seven*
Illegal Immigrants and Our Borders

107 *For Further Reading*

109 *Immigration-Related Organizations*

113 *Index*

THE NEW IMMIGRANTS

1

OUR TEEMING SHORES

"Keep, ancient lands, your storied pomp!"
cries she
With silent lips. Give me your tired, your poor,
Your huddled masses yearning to breathe free,
The wretched refuse of your teeming shore.
Send these, the homeless, tempest-tossed to me:
I lift my lamp beside the golden door!

Emma Lazarus
"The New Colossus"

A nation of immigrants"; "the melting pot of the world's peoples"—these expressions have long been used proudly by Americans to describe their country's heritage. The year 1986 marks the centennial of the Statue of Liberty, celebrated in this country and around the world as the symbol of the ideals of freedom for which this country stands. The words inscribed at its base eloquently proclaim our vision of a better life for the world's downtrodden peoples.

Today, however, the "golden door" is often spoken of as being tarnished. The deserts of the Southwest, where our border with Mexico is guarded only by the undermanned Border Patrol, are daily the scene of smuggling—of people and drugs. Our immigration officials are accused of taking bribes and of mistreating suspected illegal immigrants. Men and women desperate to enter the United States pay exorbitant fees to unscrupulous smugglers, some of whom have then left them to die in the desert. In the Caribbean waters off the coast of Florida people are crammed without food or water aboard unseaworthy boats attempting to flee political repression or poverty and begin a new life in the United States.

In the recent past hundreds of thousands of war refugees in Southeast Asia were forced to live in internment camps ill-prepared to harbor them and aboard boats in international waters, where they were attacked by pirates. No country would accept them as immigrants. We welcomed a great number of them to our shores.

Our country continues to be the goal of citizens of the world's nations who seek to start new lives in a new country, just as it was in the previous two centuries. Yet today many factors seem to indicate that indeed times and circumstances have changed from what they were in the earlier days of our nation's history, when we seemed a land unlimited in resources and optimism. Certainly the situation has changed from a century ago when we first began to formulate immigration policy. Today our immigration policy is a matter for debate among many factions, but it is by no means clear-cut.

As it has been several times before in our history, today immigration to the United States is a controversial topic. Almost everyone agrees that something must be done to gain control of a situation viewed as being totally unmanageable. But exactly what shape the reforms should take is at the center of a touchy debate. Many Americans are concerned that economic, social, and political realities of today's world may force us to restrict immigration severely—if not actually to slam shut the golden doors. But many others maintain that our immigration policy falls short of what is necessary. Human rights activists, ethnic groups, church organizations, resettlement agencies, and others believe that if we adopt a more restrictive immigration policy we will no longer live up to our self-image as a beacon of light in the darkness of human misery.

Nearly everyone, however, agrees that some changes are needed. In the U.S. Congress the call for change took the form of a highly controversial bill, the comprehensive immigration legislation known as the "Simpson-Mazzoli bill." This bill called for substantial reform of major parts of our immigration policy. It proposed fines and prison terms for employers who knowingly hire illegal aliens, legal status for illegal aliens who have lived here continuously since 1982, and easier seasonal employment of aliens by farmers during harvesting. Late in June 1984 the House of Representatives passed many of these reforms, previously passed by the Senate. Lobbying by Hispanic and civil rights groups during the presidential nominating conventions and the campaign, however, brought more political pressure to bear, and the bill was criticized by both parties' candidates. Few issues in recent years generated this kind of emotional sensitivity and passion in the public forum.

The *New York Times* described the situation this way in an editorial:

> The day for nonpartisanship is over, partisan politics is back—and immigration reform is cooked until 1985. That means America's immigration policy will continue to be a Big Wink. Illegal aliens will keep streaming in past the pitifully overworked Immigration Service. Americans will turn even more cynical, and nativist, and sentiment to curtail all immigration will continue to rise. Slam the door, people will say.

As the *Times* points out, the consensus is that, despite the controversy, we need a reasonable, fair, and enforceable immigration policy, with provisions for protecting the human rights of legal and illegal immigrants and refugees alike. Without such a policy the situation will continue to deteriorate. If as a result the restrictionist attitude prevails, Americans will be forced to "slam the door."

Hope for a New Life

And who are these people we would be shutting out? While the debate rages on in Congress and among the many diverse interest groups in this country, the personal circumstances of the immigrants and would-be immigrants themselves have not altered: the pressures for acceptance by our country for resettlement here remain strong and unyielding in the face of world politics and economic conditions. Many Americans, secure in a country where there is opportunity and freedom denied to many other nations' peoples, question why anyone would leave the country of his birth, uprooting himself from the society of friends, relations, and familiar customs, exiling himself to a land where a foreign language is spoken, or the people are of another race or practice a different religion.

Often the different social customs cause misunderstanding, and the new immigrant is not welcomed by all his new countrymen. Immigrants also suffer separation from loved ones left behind. But even when families emigrate together, the anxiety and hardship resulting from dramatically altered circumstances—even those changed for the better—can cause great stress in family relationships. Many sacrifices must be made to cope with all of these difficulties and start a successful new life. Of course, it is this hope for a better life that primarily motivates emigrants to leave their native lands. (Our language distinguishes *em*igrants and *im*migrants. Emigrants are those who leave their country for another. Immigrants are those from another country living in a new nation. In other words, a person emigrates to this country and once here becomes an immigrant.)

The lure of life in America, with its high standard of living and political freedom, exerts a strong pull on the citizens of the Third World. Whereas in the period from 1930 to 1960 about 80 percent of America's immigrants came from Europe or Canada, in only three years, from 1965 to 1968, 80 percent came from Asia and Latin America, primarily Mexico, the Philippines, Korea, China and Taiwan, Jamaica, and the Dominican Republic. What enabled those people to enter our country in such great numbers were the Immigration and Nationality Act amendments of 1965. These amendments to our immigration laws revolutionized the nature of our country's immigrant population. They abandoned the 1921 "national origins" system (based on admitting a percentage of people from a particular country on the basis of how many from that country have already settled here) that preserved the preponderance of European immigrants.

Although setting the first limits ever on the numbers that could enter from Mexico, the Caribbean, and other parts of the Western Hemisphere, the new amendments eliminated the previous limits on Eastern Hemisphere immigration. The new system was based on a new preference system. What was most dramatic about the 1965 changes was that for the first time the United States opened its doors to the racial and ethnic balance of the entire world. The result, according to chronicler Theodore White, was a "stampede, almost an invasion" of people seeking a new life here. Indeed, over the past decade and a half alone an average of one million people a year, mostly from Asia, Latin America, and the Caribbean, have come to our "teeming shores." They are Mexican-Americans like the four elected members of the San Antonio, Texas, city council; Hmong refugees (people from one of Laos's main tribes) in Providence, Rhode Island, forced to leave their homes after the Communist takeover in Southeast Asia; Vietnamese fishermen in Biloxi, Mississippi; illegal Haitian factory workers hiding from immigration agents in Brooklyn, New York; Filipino-Americans working in professional jobs in Honolulu, Hawaii; Korean-American entrepreneurs in Seattle, Washington; and Cuban-American schoolteachers in Union City, New Jersey.

Some applied for legal immigration documents from State Department officials in their countries, sometimes waiting as long as fourteen years. Others were given emergency refugee status and were flown to the United States by army transport. Some waited in camps of first asylum (in countries that admitted them temporarily to await resettlement elsewhere) for up to five years. Some arrived by spacious commercial airliner, while others stumbled out of cramped "pleasure" boats, having gone without food or water for days. Many came with tourist visas and overstayed the legal time limit. Many walked across the border under the cover of night. All are the new immigrants, and basically they fall into three overall categories:

- *Legal immigrants*—aliens (people not citizens of the United States) who have been lawfully admitted for permanent residence. They may apply for citizenship through the naturalization process and are free to pursue any work they choose. (The U.S. pullout from Vietnam after the end of the war there, in 1975, was one dramatic episode bringing many recent immigrants from Southeast Asia.)

- *Refugees*—persons who are unwilling or unable to return to their countries of origin because of persecution on account of race, religion, nationality, membership in a particular group, or political opinion. (Over half a million refugees from Indochina have been admitted since 1975; many fled the aftermath of destruction that followed the Vietnam War. Also, in 1980 at least 155,000 Cubans and Haitians were paroled into the country by President Carter but not given refugee status. Many more flee repressive regimes throughout the world daily.)

- *Illegal immigrants*—undocumented or deportable aliens who have violated the immigration law by entering the country illegally, bypassing inspection, or by overstaying the terms of legal entry. They are not permitted to work legally in this country. (No one knows exactly how many are here, but signs of their presence are everywhere. The tide continues to be more than the Immigration and Naturalization Service can handle, especially at the Mexican border.)

Whether they entered legally as those admitted by the 1965 amendments to the immigration laws, legally as refugees admitted by the Refugee Act of 1980 or as "special entrants" permitted here by presidential decree, or illegally as aliens without visas or work papers, all of these people are those we call the new immigrants. All have changed our country's character and look.

America's Changing Society

With the entry of these new immigrants, our society has grown dramatically. It now includes those of every ethnic culture, a microcosm of the world in one country. Since the founding of this country each successive ethnic group that has established itself here has warned of the dangers imposed by incoming aliens changing the national character. First the British and Dutch Protestants opposed Irish, French, and Spanish Catholics. Both groups then warned of Eastern and Central European Jews. Northern Europeans were wary of Southern Europeans changing America. Racial hostility was directed against Italians, Slavs, and Eastern European Jews.

Today, because of the changes in our immigration policy, people of color—Asians, Latin Americans, Caribbeans—are the main groups changing our country's makeup. And this change brings with it difficult adjustments. Unease about ethnic differences has always been part of our response to new immigrants.

Cultural differences today's new immigrants bring with them mean our country is developing a new culture, an amalgam of the old European with the new Asian and Hispanic influences. What are our concerns about these changes? The newcomers all bring unfamiliar religious practices, languages, family traditions, eating and drinking habits, sexual practices, work styles, and social behavior. Most Americans are puzzled and uncertain about these differences. Although we know little about their cultures and traditions, we are interested and curious for the most part. Unlike the early American groups who cast aspersion and suspicion on incoming nationalities, on the whole we accept, and often welcome, the new. Most clashes between the old and the new have involved preserving what we need to survive, as in the case of jobs, for example. The main group Americans expressed nearly universal disdain for were the small number of prisoners and mental patients Fidel Castro sent to Miami in 1980, along with those in the boatlift from the port of Mariel to Miami, after those seeking to leave Cuba took over the Peruvian embassy in Havana.

Certain areas of the country have had to make greater adjustments to the new immigrants than others have. Southern Florida is first on the list of those most affected. In one year alone Florida received 125,000 Cubans and Haitians. Los Angeles, California, is another area that has been changed by the new immigrants. It has received a large Mexican population as well as many Asians. And a third area that has been greatly affected by the new immigrants is Texas. The Mexican border—cities such as Laredo and Del Rio—houses Mexicans in great numbers. But for the most part the new immigrants of the past decade have settled throughout the country and have been undergoing a process of gradual assimilation, becoming Americans and adjusting to our way of life as we adjust to their presence and the changes they bring.

Continuing the American Dream

Although times have changed since the early immigrants to the United States helped create the country's reputation as a land where hard work, determination, and a little luck are the keys to the American dream of success, some new immigrants are proving that it still can be done.

Lawyer Luis Gómez-Domínquez, fifty-nine, came from Cuba to the United States in 1979. His first job was cutting grass in a city park in Miami. Today Gómez-Domínquez is a marketing manager for the city, promoting and developing Miami's assets to business, industry, and the public. "My family and friends helped me," he said. "But the real thing was that I began to work hard immediately."

James Kong, thirty-nine, and his wife Han are Koreans who arrived in Chicago in 1976. At first they each worked two jobs until they saved enough to buy the tailoring shop where Mrs. Kong worked as a seamstress. Today the Kongs own five dry-cleaning stores and a wholesale plant. "We have to work harder and longer hours or we wouldn't make the opportunities," said Mr. Kong.

Dung Anh Do arrived in Denver in 1977 from Vietnam. He worked as a janitor, a truck driver, and in other low-paying jobs until he was able to turn a part-time printing and copying business into Lion Press. The first month in operation he earned twelve thousand dollars in the business.

Another Vietnamese, Mai Tran, thirty-one, sold most of her possessions, pooled money with a relative, and borrowed eleven thousand dollars from friends to buy a small cafe in San Francisco. "So far we are contributing our time and dollars for nothing," she said. "But it is worthwhile. We are building something here."

These success stories are echoed by many others who have come as new immigrants. But of course there are less encouraging reports too. The American dream is far from the grasp of unskilled, undocumented aliens in the United States illegally, like the migrant fruit pickers in the West or sweatshop workers in the East. And some refugees from rural countries such as Laos or Haiti have had even more trouble finding a niche in our urban society. How the new immigrants are responding to life in the United States and how our country's citizens are being affected by their presence is not one story but many, with a full, diverse cast of characters, many dissimilar settings, and frequent twists of plot, told from many points of view.

In the following pages we will look at the experiences of some immigrants to our country and see in greater detail why they chose, or were forced, to seek a new life. We will try to understand some of the ways that these immigrants have affected us as a nation, as a society. And we will examine some of the issues—political, social, economic, and humanitarian—that must be addressed as our country struggles to shape a new immigration policy to take us into the twenty-first century.

2

LEGAL IMMIGRANTS: HISPANICS AND ASIANS

I hereby declare, on oath, that I absolutely and entirely renounce and abjure all allegiance and fidelity to any foreign prince, potentate, state or sovereignty, of whom or which I have heretofore been a subject or citizen; that I will support and defend the Constitution and laws of the United States of America against all enemies, foreign and domestic; that I will bear true faith and allegiance to the same; that I will bear arms on behalf of the United States when required by law; that I will perform noncombatant service in the armed forces of the United States when required by law; that I will perform work of national importance under civilian direction when required by law; and that I take this obligation freely without any mental reservation or purpose of evasion; so help me God.

U.S. Citizenship Petition Oath

Most of the newcomers who have been legally admitted as immigrants under the 1965 changes to our immigration laws are Hispanics and Asians. These two largest categories also include those who have come as refugees, as well as those who have come (or overstayed) illegally. Although many varying cultural groups make up these two ethnic categories, together they represent the major forces changing American culture.

A Rich Tapestry of Hispanic Culture

Currently Hispanics (Spanish-speaking Cubans, Central and South Americans, Mexicans, and Latinos from the Caribbean) are the second largest and fastest-growing minority in the United States. Hispanics live in every state in the Union, but well over half are concentrated in Arizona, California, Colorado, New Mexico, and Texas. Many also live in Florida. Although they are united by their Spanish language and Catholic religion, the different groups also exhibit unique differences. Their heritage is a rich tapestry of Spanish, Indian, mulatto, and Afro-American influences.

Hispanics made up about 6.3 percent of the general population in 1980 but represented only 3.5 percent of the work force. Many Hispanic workers are not represented in that figure, however, because they work illegally, as undocumented aliens. Statistics reveal that Hispanics are among the lowest paid, poorest housed, and least educated of the ethnic minority groups.

Despite the problems they face in our culture, Hispanics will have a great impact on the future of the United States, as indicated by the following trends:

- Hispanics are projected to become the largest minority during the 1980s.

- Already the fourth largest Spanish-speaking nation in this hemisphere, the United States is projected to become the third largest by 1990. Spanish is the second most frequently spoken language in this country.
- In 1990 about half of California's residents and a third of Texas' may be Spanish speaking; Hispanics could be the majority in three or four states.
- The future safety and economic health of the United States are interdependent with those of Mexico and Latin America.
- The second largest group of Hispanics found anywhere in the world lives in Los Angeles; by 1999 most people living there will probably have Spanish surnames, according to *Futurist* magazine.
- The Hispanic market is one of the fastest growing in the United States, with household purchasing power of $31 billion in 1978.
- Nearly half of the total U.S. Hispanic population is now under twenty-one; they will come to political and economic strength during the late 1980s and the 1990s.

Clearly the Hispanic influence on our culture is growing. Unemployment, failing economies, and unstable, sometimes repressive governments, in Mexico, Latin America, and the Caribbean will continue to make the United States a desirable new home for those who aspire to a better life, where employment, higher pay, and political freedom are all offered to most who pursue them.

Hispanics have come from every country in Central and South America and from every social class in those countries. They constitute a proud, hard-working, and culturally rich part of our society. Their contribution to our country has been great. Yet one current social phenomenon particularly affects Hispanic-Americans along with the rest of the members of our society—the growth in number of illegal aliens, or undocumented workers, from Mexico and Latin America. This trend threatens both groups; it is the centerpiece of much of the controversy about our present immigration policy. (This pressing issue is discussed in more detail later in the book.)

Cubans Revitalizing Decaying Cities

Cubans are one of the diverse Hispanic groups changing our country. The first Cubans who immigrated to the United States were educated, middle-class citizens who fled Fidel Castro's revolution in the early 1960s. These Cubans have settled in every state, adapting remarkably well to their new country. The largest and best-known Cuban U.S. community is Miami, which the Cubans have revitalized. They transformed decaying areas and boosted the city's economy, making it an international center some call the "capital of Latin America." The success of the Cubans who came to the United States in the 1960s and 1970s and of Miami's transformation is well known.

Less publicized but equally impressive are the changes the Cubans helped bring about in northern Hudson County, New Jersey, in and near Union City. This urban area was fast becoming a sprawl of slums. More than eighty thousand Cubans settled here, making it the second largest Cuban community after Miami. They transformed entire neighborhoods, giving new life to homes, churches, schools, and businesses. In 1980 the dramatic events of the Mariel boatlift brought over 125,000 Cubans to the United States when Castro was pressured to permit all who wished to to leave the country after dissidents took over the Peruvian embassy in Havana, seeking asylum. The strong Cuban community in New Jersey responded by raising much of a $2 million fund collected to aid the Mariel refugees. The refugees found a welcome in this once-dying urban area and have helped to rescue it from decay in return.

New Areas Attracting the New Immigrants

Although the stories of Cubans revitalizing Miami and northern New Jersey cities are definite plusses for the United States, urban areas are by no means the only places the new immigrants call home. Not only are the countries of origin of the newcomers different from those of the early-twentieth-century immigrants, but also a remarkable change has occurred in where and how our foreign-born permanent residents and citizens live and work.

Most new immigrants, primarily Hispanics and Asians, no longer congregate exclusively in large American cities. Like most of our population, they have chosen to live in the suburbs or small communities of the nation's interior. A good number are professionals or skilled workers who hold good jobs and fit easily into middle-class life.

Figures from the 1980 census indicate that almost as many legal immigrants live in the suburbs as in the central cities. The big coastal cities of New York, San Francisco, and Miami still hold the highest numbers, but the suburbs are close behind. In fact, today the suburbs are more accessible to immigrants than they are to native black and Hispanic groups. They supply far more jobs and higher incomes than all the large cities. From Los Angeles and San Francisco many new immigrants have found their way into fast-growing areas of the Southeast and Mountain states, particularly immigrants from China, the Philippines, Japan, South Korea, and Vietnam, whose numbers almost doubled in the 1970s.

Asians Seeking New Life

Some of the same kinds of forces—failing economies and political instability or repression—that brought so many Hispanics to this country in recent years also encouraged or forced Asians to seek a new life here. They include those settling in suburbs and those taking over decaying areas of cities, professionals and blue-collar workers, literate city dwellers and uneducated tribespeople, those who chose to come and those who were forced out of their homes by war or political persecution.

Dr. Anthony Chu, a Chinese-born expert on snake venom, is an example of an Asian who found a home away from the big cities that historically housed immigrants—in Fort Collins, Colorado, where he is on the faculty of Colorado State University. Professor Chu was educated at Taiwan University, Notre Dame, Stanford, and Yale. He is one of twenty other Nationalist Chinese scholars on the faculty at Colorado State. Although Chu is among a small minority of foreigners in the Fort Collins area, their numbers have more than doubled in the past ten years. Most are in the professions or own businesses, ranging from karate schools to restaurants.

Koreans on West Coast

Many of the Asians who have come here legally in the past two decades are Koreans. With the 1965 change in U.S. immigration policy, the numbers of Koreans coming to this country as legal immigrants increased dramatically. From 1965 to 1970, twenty-four thousand Koreans entered the United States, including many professional people. These immigrants were generally between the ages of twenty and forty-four and had more education than any other ethnic-minority immigrants. Most settled on the West Coast, especially in California. They joined those who had come during and after the Korean War and the approximately sixty-two thousand who were admitted on temporary visas, mostly students who decided to petition the government to let them stay here as permanent residents after completing their educations in this country. In the 1970s the numbers grew larger; from 1970 to 1975, 122,000 Koreans were granted legal entry to the United States. They cited as reasons for coming the better education and job opportunities here.

The 1980 Census showed a U.S. Korean population of 354,000, five times the number recorded in 1970. Koreans thus became the fourth largest Asian group in America (after Chinese, Filipinos, and Japanese). What brought these people, many of whom were educated and skilled, to this country? As in many other countries of immigrant origin, undesirable political and social conditions seem to have been the impetus.

The Lee family, who emigrated from Korea in 1970, is typical of many Asian families who have emigrated here in the past fifteen years. David Lee, who came here with his wife Sue, explains why they and many others like them fled Korea: "From 1961 to 1979, President Park Chung-Lee's government was repressive. . . . There was martial law and censorship. Job opportunities were promised but not always available to everyone. We came to live in a free society that would allow us to have better lives."

David and Sue Lee, both twenty-two years old in 1970, had just married when they left their home near Seoul for Los Angeles. They had few problems in receiving approval from the State Department, since David's older brother Sam, fifteen years his senior, had come to this country in the early 1950s to study dentistry and had then asked to be allowed to stay. He had become a U.S. citizen in 1959. The fact that they were both educated and knew some English contributed to the Lees' easy acceptance. David had studied to be a pharmacist in Korea, and Sue had taken bookkeeping courses after high school. As relatives of a U.S. citizen and future professionals who would contribute to this country, they fit the category of preferred immigrants created by the 1965 amendments.

The Lees settled in Los Angeles, in Koreatown, a five-square-mile neighborhood in the Olympic area near the heart of the city. Approximately 150,000 Koreans live there and form a well-established support system. Seventy-two Korean churches, mostly Protestant, serve the community, along with alumni associations, trade groups, and many Korean-owned businesses. Despite the good educational background of Koreatown's residents (72 percent held professional or managerial jobs in Korea), unemployment is higher than the national average.

Although David Lee had been trained as a pharmacist in Korea (like about three hundred other Koreans in southern California at the time), he was unable to find a job when he first arrived in Koreatown. Because he was not educated in the United States, he was not permitted to take the exams for licensing pharmacists, even though his English was good. Many other Koreans educated and trained in Korea have problems obtaining work in their professions because of language problems involved in certification. Like them, David found he would have to start at the bottom of the ladder: He got a job as an orderly in a municipal hospital and after six months was given a job as a clerk in the hospital pharmacy. Sue worked as a typist in a Korean-owned travel agency; at night she attended college classes in accounting. Since

David could not follow his chosen career, he decided, like many other Asians in the United States, to save money to start a business. Sue's accounting would help. He found a Korean investor—his brother Sam. After talking to many other Koreatown businessmen, David decided to buy a shoe store that was for sale at a good price. Through his work at the hospital, he had discovered that he enjoyed working with people and serving the public. This new investment would give him a career and a chance to serve the Korean community too.

For the first two years he and Sue worked day and night to get the business off the ground. Slowly they began to pay off the mortgage and the loan from Sam. Sue worked extra hours doing accounting for other businesses. She also was able to study for her degree and public accountant's certification (CPA). After five years in Los Angeles the Lees had a business of their own that began to make a little money. They were able to hire other immigrants to work in the store.

Sue became a CPA in 1977 and set up an office above the shoe store. When she became pregnant with their first child, she and David began to work toward getting their U.S. citizenship. The baby would automatically be a citizen at birth; they too wanted to become naturalized, just as Sam had been. They studied U.S. history together and took a course in the Constitution at a local high school. Soon after their son was born they took the citizenship oath with other immigrants at the Los Angeles courthouse. Now they had truly become Americans.

Today the Lees have two sons, six and four years old, and a daughter sixteen months old. They still run the shoe store, but they moved from Koreatown to a house in a Los Angeles suburb. Their dedication to hard work and close cooperation are themes found in many Korean families who have come to this country. As David says,

"It wasn't easy for us but we are happy now. We want to be good Americans."

Filipinos—A Misunderstood Culture

The diversity of Asian cultures in the United States can be seen in the stories of Filipino immigrants. The second wave of Philippine immigration began when our immigration laws were revised in 1952. Roughly 2,500 Filipinos (a Malay people even though the Philippines are geographically part of South Asia) entered the United States each year from 1952 to 1965. After the new immigration quotas of 1965, their numbers increased until by 1970 thirty thousand a year came to settle in the cities of Los Angeles, Honolulu, Chicago, and New York. Nearly eight hundred thousand Filipinos in the United States today make them America's second largest group of Asians (after the Chinese). They were led to emigrate largely because of inflation, injustices, corruption, and poverty perpetuated by the Philippine government of President Ferdinand Marcos.

Many of the newer Filipino immigrants are professionals or students in medical or technical fields. Formerly most were unskilled workers, many of whom labored as farm workers on the West Coast or as maids and maintenance workers in homes and hospitals in cities. In 1965 Filipinos merged with Mexican-American union members organized by Cesar Chavez to form the United Farm Workers. The fact that Filipinos are predominantly Catholic, speak Spanish, and have Spanish surnames and yet come from Asia confuses many Americans who are not aware of the Spanish domination of the Philippines for four hundred years. As one Filipino immigrant says, "We are confused with Chicanos."

It is partly that confusion and partly the characteristics of Filipino culture in the United States that has kept Filipinos in the background among immigrant groups in this country, overshadowed by other Asian groups who present a clearer image to Americans. Unlike the Chinese and Japanese, who have established large support organizations in this country and are so visible with their restaurants, electronics companies, and Oriental cultural traditions, the Filipinos are often overlooked. Many Filipino immigrants here think that will change; they hope the newer, more educated arrivals will establish Filipino culture in America and raise their voices to proclaim the identity of the Filipino community.

All New Asian Groups Populate New York's Boroughs

Filipinos are joined by the other new Asians in New York's boroughs of Queens, the Bronx, and Brooklyn. There Vietnamese, Cambodians (now their country is called Kampuchea), Laotians, Thais, Koreans, Filipinos, Chinese, and some Japanese throng the streets at rush hours. A half-century before they were preceded by settlers from Europe. Some estimate that today more than four hundred thousand Asian Americans live in the city. They have made parts of New York, some run down and left vacant by previous immigrant groups, their own. No longer crowded into Chinatown exclusively, they are spread throughout the metropolis.

On Main Street in Flushing, Queens, one of the most urban areas of the highly urbanized East Coast, where concrete and asphalt, steel and iron, dominate the landscape, Korean vegetable and fruit stores and gift shops prosper. Many of the shoppers are Asians. More than twenty thousand of New York's eighty thousand Koreans live there now, and nine thousand new Koreans join them each year. Nearly eighty-five hundred Asian students attend the New York City university system.

And in public schools in Queens alone the number of Asian students tripled from 1970 to 1980. A Korean woman says, "In 1964 when I came here to school, it was so hard to find a Korean store in New York. . . . Now there are grocery stores, vegetable stores, all the shops."

The boroughs of the Bronx and Brooklyn, where rents are generally lower than New York's Manhattan and Queens neighborhoods, also have new immigrants as residents. Many from Indochina and mainland China arrive without knowledge of English and must at first take low-paying jobs in restaurants and small factories and live where rents are lowest. Some landlords and employers say they would have few takers for these apartments and jobs: "The immigrants will take these so they can save and buy a business of their own." And as Cac Thanh Le, a Vietnamese studying to be a doctor, says, "You do not know you are so lucky. We have a four-room apartment here, much better than the studio in Saigon." When asked how immigrants tolerate tenement apartments, Maureen Sui, who emigrated from Hong Kong five years ago, answered that in Hong Kong "some people must rent bed space on eight-hour shifts. When your time is up, they wake you so the next person can have the bed."

The Asians' neighbors see them as a stabilizing influence. Many New Yorkers buy produce from the vegetable stores, flowers from the shops, and food at the restaurants. They feel the Asians add an interesting mix of Oriental cultures to the city. They are not worried that the neighborhoods will become "Koreatowns" or like Manhattan's Chinatown, pushing all others out. "There are many other ethnic groups as well. The days of Chinatown are over," one said. Another added: "The [Asian] people take such good care of their houses and their businesses."

Asian immigrants and their Hispanic counterparts are finding new ways of settling in the United States. They are making the cities new again and discovering America's suburbs. In their struggle to become new Americans, they are affected by two issues—bilingualism and upward mobility. The first concerns their use of English as their dominant language in the United States for education and business; the second involves whether this country enables them to have a chance to succeed, considering their drive and access to those attributes that determine success or failure in a culture. Both these issues—and how they affect the new immigrants—are discussed in the next chapter.

3

BILINGUALISM AND UPWARD MOBILITY

We have room in this country for
but one flag, the Stars and Stripes. . . .
We have room for but one loyalty,
loyalty to the United States. . . .
We have room for but one language,
the English language.

Theodore Roosevelt
The Great Adventure

Two of the most relevant issues for the new immigrants and our country today are those that concern our language, English, and the opportunities for upward mobility—the chance to get ahead. In one area of American life the effects of immigration in the last twenty years can be seen and heard more obviously than in any other. That area is our language: it is no longer just in the ethnic neighborhoods of our largest cities that the voices of other nations can be heard. In practically every city and in most suburban areas and even in many small towns, speakers of "foreign" languages can be heard on street corners, in buses, on playgrounds, and in supermarkets.

Historically, the pressure to assimilate and to get ahead in the American mainstream has encouraged immigrants to learn English. This is the path that most immigrants and their descendants have taken, and the United States has remained a country that speaks only one language in public affairs and in the marketplace of national and international business.

Today the pattern of immigration has changed and has resulted in a greater concentration of immigrants speaking the same language than ever before in our history. Although the figures are not exact, it is apparent that more than half of all immigrants coming to the United States share one language—Spanish. In the past fifteen years more than 40 percent of all legal immigration came from Latin America, and, it is thought, one-half of all illegal immigration comes from Mexico. Additional immigrants come from other Spanish-speaking countries such as the Philippines.

Supreme Court Decision

In 1974, in a landmark decision the Supreme Court declared that children who do not understand English are entitled to special educational programs to overcome this difficulty. In this decision, *Lau v. Nichols*, the court stated, "there is no equality of treatment merely by providing students with the same facilities, textbooks, teachers, and curriculum, for students who do not understand English are effectively foreclosed from any meaningful education."

The case of *Lau v. Nichols* was brought by the parents of a Chinese-speaking child, but the decision granting the right of a "meaningful education" to non-English-speaking students had its widest application to those who speak Spanish. The Court did not specifically mandate bilingual education as the remedy, saying, "No specific remedy is urged upon us. Teaching English to the students of Chinese ancestry is one choice. Giving instructions to this group in Chinese is another. There may be others."

In the view of many Hispanic teachers, lawyers, social workers, and cultural activists, however, Spanish-language education was the desired remedy. Subsequent court-mandated bilingual education programs proliferated, and Congress passed the Bilingual Education Act to legislate funding for them. Most programs involved Spanish-speaking children.

In addition to bilingualism in schools, certain areas of the country (those with language minority groups that total more than 5 percent of the voters) must provide bilingual ballots, according to a 1975 amendment to the Voting Rights Act. Hispanics are not the only group to avail themselves of this right, but their size in numbers and the insistence of Hispanic social activists tend to make many other Americans feel that Hispanics do not want to play by the same "rules" of assimilation that have been followed by immigrants in the past. They fear that bilingualism promotes cultural disunity and that this could lead to cultural separatism, as in Canada, where French-speaking factions and English-speaking ones are frequently at odds. At issue, they feel, is the very unity of our country, socially and politically.

Bilingual education in itself can and probably should be considered on its merits and demerits as an educational tool. If it serves strictly as an aid to students who would do poorly without it, then it may have value. The evidence so far has not clearly demonstrated its effectiveness one way or the other.

Some native Spanish speakers who acquired their English mastery the old "sink or swim" way on their own feel that the rigors it imposed and the attitudes needed to overcome the obstacle may have helped them to learn English better and faster. On the other hand, they say that the trauma and emotional intimidation involved in being plunged into an incomprehensible school program is destructive for other children who cannot handle this challenge. These children grow up feeling inadequate in both languages. Most immigrants, now and in the past, say that having the opportunity to ease into English with a transitional period of native language classes aided their adaptation to the new environment. But is this the case, or does it reflect the desire for the comfort of the familiar and safe? Others have admitted that trading off being forced to learn English for emotional security would be preferable but might delay mastering the new language—perhaps permanently. Statistical or other objective measurements are not adequate to settle the issue. Each approach may be appropriate in different situations with particular children. Nevertheless, it appears that most Spanish-speaking parents and children believe that the way to get ahead in our society is to master the English language, and this is what they are doing.

Spanish as a Symbol

Perhaps the larger and root issue in this debate is the matter of Hispanic pride and the desire of many new immigrants to maintain Hispanic culture in the United States. Through the 1950s immigrants who wanted to preserve their culture while living and working as Americans had a difficult time. As one pro-Hispanic advocate points out in the journal *Migration Today*, "After World War I . . . the U.S. turned resolutely inward, and bilingual education, which smacked of decadent Europe, was abolished in the public schools. The conventional wisdom of the day was that bilingualism was a handicap and that assimilation required eradication of the immigrants' native cultures and languages as quickly as possible."

In the 1960s and 1970s America as a society, however, seemed to lose the domineering sense of national identity necessary to continue to impose English as a national language on all newcomers. Certainly the protection of children's educational rights and of voters' access to the polls were laudable intentions. But the questions remain: Is the Hispanic insistence on maintaining cultural identity a threat to America's national identity? Is the preservation of English as a national language necessary to our social and political unity?

Some Hispanic advocates of bilingualism believe that with an ever growing Spanish-speaking population it is inevitable that at some time in the future the United States would become a two-language nation, that Spanish will have all the legal status that English has had heretofore, with all public and economic affairs conducted in both languages. But an opposing group feels that indeed limited bilingualism in schools and on voting ballots may be carrying the United States down that road, and it is time to put a halt to bilingualism before this happens. Such public interest groups as U.S. English, a Washington-based lobby group headed by an Eastern European immigrant now a U.S. citizen, believe that having only one official language is absolutely necessary to maintain the common bond that keeps us unified as a nation. S. I.

Hayakawa, the former U.S. senator and a professor of linguistics, is spearheading a drive to have a constitutional amendment passed declaring English the sole official language of the United States.

There are no easy answers to these questions. Well-intentioned citizens with this country's best interests at heart can be found on both sides of the issue. The majority opinion is probably that tolerance and accommodation must be practiced by all concerned. It is often pointed out that *Hispanic* is an all-inclusive term that is too loosely used. The cultures, beliefs, and opinions of Cuban-Americans, Mexican-Americans, Puerto Ricans (who are of course native Americans), Filipinos, Salvadorans, and other "Hispanic" peoples are not all identical, or even similar. Although they are beginning to join forces politically, as with the Hispanic Caucus in Congress, there are wide differences among Hispanics; in some instances almost all they have in common is their language.

Upward Mobility

Immigrants' ability to get into the American mainstream of economic success seems to be holding as true for today's immigrants, as it did for generations past. In a government study researchers found that immigrant families started to earn more than native-born American families within ten years, on average, after arriving in this country. They also found that, even with the added burden of adapting to learning in another language, the children of immigrants equal the academic performance of children of native-born families. After an initial period of being at a disadvantage, they tended to overtake the native-born group in terms of years of schooling and percentage of children completing college.

Part of the reason for the rapid approach to equality

is the age and education of the newcomers. They tend to be young people with few children, and their prime working years are ahead of them. Another reason for their relatively high achievement is that they tend to be highly motivated people who are perhaps the survivors in a kind of natural selection process. Some social theorists believe that the emigration process is weighted in favor of those individuals who are resourceful and determined. People who are comfortable, or merely passive, do not choose to undergo the rigors of immigration. Those who are too weak or incapable cannot overcome the obstacles in the way of getting to the new land.

The characteristic positive traits of many immigrants are referred to as the "immigrant personality." They are ambitious and willing to take a risk. They have the knowledge or the cleverness to devise a plan, raise the money, and carry it through. These capabilities serve them well after arrival. It may be that they benefit from the experiences they go through and are wiser and tougher for them. These experiences and attitudes apparently also motivate immigrant parents to invest their concern in their children's schooling, producing a high level of academic achievement.

Available data seem to support the theory that refugees may have a harder time and take longer to adjust successfully than other immigrants. This may be because they are forced by political events to migrate, and thus they are not self-selected for the favorable traits of the immigrant personality, the most important of which is the willingness to adapt. In the next three chapters we look at the refugees and their problems, where they come from as well as why and how, and the issues they and our country confront as they become Americans.

4

REFUGEES: INDOCHINESE EXODUS

A refugee would like to have your problems.

United Nations
Human Rights
Commission slogan

According to the United Nations, more than two thousand people per day attempt to flee from persecution in their own countries in Southeast Asia, Afghanistan, the Soviet Union, Cuba, Africa, Central America, and many other troubled parts of the world. The United States plays an enormous role in aiding and resettling these homeless persons. More than 600,000 Indochinese have come to America since 1975, and 125,000 Cubans came in 1980 alone. The 1980 bill to the federal government for refugee aid topped one billion dollars.

Refugee Act of 1980

The Refugee Act of 1980 was enacted as an amendment to the Immigration and Nationality Act, with two basic purposes in mind: One was to provide a procedure for the annual admission of refugees to the United States, and for their admission in emergency situations; and the second was to authorize federal assistance to resettle refugees and to promote their self-sufficiency. Basically, the act formalized the U.S. position on refugees, ending the ad hoc approach that had characterized our refugee policy since World War II.

The impact of large numbers of refugees in the last ten years has caused considerable controversy and raised the important questions, What is a refugee? Whom should we admit to this category, entitling them to all the benefits it confers?

The 1980 law set an annual numerical limit (allocated among refugee groups by the president after consultation with Congress) on refugee admission to the United States. The refugee ceiling for 1984, for example, was set at 72,000, allotted as follows: Africa, 3,000; East Asia, 50,000; Eastern Europe and the Soviet Union,

12,000; Latin America and the Caribbean, 1,000; and the Near East and South Asia, 6,000.

The act adopted the UN's definition of a refugee, which is a person outside his or her country of nationality, fearing return to that country because of persecution or a well-founded fear of persecution on account of race, religion, nationality, political opinion, or membership in a social group.

The previous U.S. criterion was that a refugee had to be from a Communist-dominated or Middle Eastern country. The broader UN definition seems more humanitarian, but according to some analysts, it creates a problem of interpretation. Some are concerned that people who voluntarily leave their countries for economic reasons are not, but should be, excluded from the UN definition. Unemployment and even starvation are widespread in many developing countries. Some Americans fear that an overwhelming tide of such people could gain entry to our shores by claiming refugee status. After all, a case can be made that economic well-being is no less fundamental to human life than fears of persecution. People who feel this way argue that there is nothing voluntary about being forced to leave your country because you cannot make enough money for your family to survive. They believe that "economic" refugees are just as deserving of our help as "persecuted" refugees. It is hard to see, however, by what criteria the United States could select whom to admit from among the many millions who might in the future attempt to come here for economic reasons. The alternative would be a return to the open-door policy of entry for all.

The question of who is a refugee also has political implications. Some people charge that those who flee from countries whose governments the United States supports, such as Haiti and El Salvador, are sometimes refused entry as refugees because the United States does not wish to offend these governments by suggesting that they persecute their citizens.

Help for the Needy

The 1980 Refugee Act recognizes that because refugees are fleeing for their very lives, they are temporarily dependent on others for their survival, and they need and deserve help. The act provides the mechanism for coordinating and financing this aid until the refugees can become self-sufficient. It also recognizes the federal government's responsibility to relieve state and local governments of the financial burden of federal refugee policies.

Senator Alan Simpson (R-Wy), chairman of the Senate Subcommittee on Immigration and Refugee Policy, has called our refugee resettlement efforts of the past decade a "bright achievement." Some of the changes these efforts brought to the lives of new Americans are apparent when we look at the stories of some of the refugees themselves. In the next section we look at the Indochinese refugees who fled their countries during and after the Vietnam War—how they left and why, what happened to them when they got there, and how they are adapting to life in their new country. Then, after that, we look at the situation for some other refugees—from Cuba, El Salvador, Haiti, and the Soviet Union. Even though they come from different areas of the world, as refugees they share many of the same experiences and difficulties in adjusting to a new society; some also share the same triumphs.

Massive Exodus

The fall of Saigon to the North Vietnamese Communists in April 1975 signaled the start of a massive exodus of

Indochinese refugees, not only from South Vietnam but also from Cambodia (now Kampuchea) and Laos. Many fled the Communist takeover because of their political or religious beliefs; many who had helped the United States during the war feared for their lives if they stayed. The United States had prepared for the exodus when the outcome of the fighting became clear. The government alerted the UN and other international organizations of the impending crisis for the refugees. It then used its legal emergency authority to admit persons whose lives were believed to be in danger, granted under the 1965 immigration reforms.

Evacuations by air and boat were quickly staged by the U.S. government, which transported 130,000 Vietnamese, Laotians, and Cambodians (Kampucheans) in the last days of April 1975 directly to this country or to temporary transit centers in Guam and the Philippines.

An interagency government task force set about resettling the refugees in this country. Private voluntary organizations, mostly based in churches, supported the immense task of resettlement. They found sponsors who would assist refugees individually, arrange for transportation to the refugees' new home towns, and watch over the refugees until they were self-supporting.

The government task force quickly opened reception areas at military bases in California, Florida, Arkansas, and Pennsylvania. Fort Chaffee, in Arkansas, the largest of the reception areas, stayed open until December 1975. In less than eight months, 130,000 Vietnamese and 5,000 Cambodians had been given sponsors and resettled in communities throughout the country.

Unlike the Others

These new refugees were unlike any other group resettled in the past in this country. They were Orientals whisked almost overnight into a Western country they knew little about. Few spoke any English. Many were from illiterate, rural tribes. The hard work, experience, and close cooperation of the voluntary agencies, teamed with the government's quick actions and commitment of resources, made early rescue efforts an exhilarating success. After the failures of the Vietnam War, these experiences helped in small part to redeem our nation's self-esteem.

The success of the first evacuations was followed later in 1975 by a flow of refugees from Laos, many of whom were from the Hmong tribe, hill people who were in danger of being persecuted or killed because of their different race and their history of cooperation with the United States in its military efforts during the war. More refugees from throughout Indochina followed, and the flow continued unabated. Members of all classes fled Vietnam, Cambodia, and Laos. Some, like the Khmer from Cambodia, had their homes and farmland destroyed in their country. Others, like the ethnic Chinese, had been expelled from Vietnam, their adopted home for centuries, by the Communists.

Those who fled by land, the "land people" from Kampuchea (Cambodia's present name) and from Laos (primarily the Hmong and Mien) crossed the border on foot into Thailand, where they were put into camps to await resettlement elsewhere. (Thailand is a country of "first asylum," one that agrees to receive but not resettle the refugees; countries of "second asylum," such as the United States, accept for permanent resettlement refugees who have been granted asylum in other countries first.) From 1975 to 1979 more than 450,000 land people took this route.

The Boat People

If the flight of the land people was one of struggle and fear, that of the "boat people," those who fled clandestinely by sea, was no less dangerous and difficult. The boat people from Vietnam fled in 1975 at the end of the war to any noncommunist nation they could reach that would accept them. The following year their plight became known to the world. At first the boat people were primarily ethnic Vietnamese leaving by stealth in small fishing boats unsuited for the high seas. Perhaps 30 percent of them perished at sea or were captured by the Communist Vietnamese. Pirates preyed on the small boats. Some ports turned them away. Some ship captains ignored the international law of the seas requiring them to assist other ships in distress, to rescue passengers and crew and carry them to the first port of call.

Later, as the Communist government in Hanoi intensified its drive to eliminate ethnic Chinese in Vietnam, whom they deemed undesirable, large vessels capable of carrying several thousand refugees left Vietnam under government supervision. At great expense those who chose to leave paid an exit fee to the government and in many cases a bribe to a middleman, often in gold.

The stories of the land people and the boat people who survived are full of danger, loss of family, fear, loneliness, isolation, hunger, illness, torture and extortion by captors, and extreme disorientation at being faced with a strange culture so foreign to their own. Many were required to spend years in inadequate camps in countries of first asylum. The flights from their homelands constituted one of history's most dramatic events.

Many of the refugees had stories similar to those of the Chang family who fled Laos.

Family Flees with Entire Village

Joua Chang was used to war, like nearly all the men of his tribe, the Hmong of Laos. A northern mountain-dwelling people, the Hmong men are known for their farming, silversmithing, and hunting, and the women for their beautiful embroidery and sewing. Joua had fought against the Communists all his life. Because the Hmong had helped the United States by fighting as guerrillas in defense of their land and rescuing many downed U.S. pilots, they were singled out for persecution and extermination by the Communist Pathet Lao party, which took over Laos after Indochina fell in 1975. Their homes and villages were burned. Thousands of Hmong men, women and children were killed. Thousands more fled the destruction and death.

It was nearly midnight in the small village. Joua Chang's wife, Her My, tightened the small woven bags of herbs around the ankles and wrists of her three children. She prayed that the spirits would protect them. The two boys, Vang and Chu, ran to their father, who gave them bags of rice to carry on their backs. Her My hoisted the baby girl Youa onto her back in the traditional Hmong style. Like her neighbors, she and her family also carried a plastic cover to protect them from the rain. Joua carried the tent he had used as a soldier.

Just five hours earlier the entire village, more than a thousand men, women, and children, had gathered on the road that led to their village near Sayaboury, Laos. In small groups they shared information about their situation. They knew many villages nearby had been destroyed. Finally they decided: they would start tonight. First by foot to the Mekong River separating Laos from Thailand, then by raft to cross to the safety of Thailand, and then, they knew not how, to the United States. They spread word of the decision from one family to the next. Then they hurried off to gather the food, clothing, and supplies they would need. In a few hours they began their flight from Laos, once called the Kingdom of a Million Elephants, now ravaged and split by war.

Each night the Chang family put up their small tent and built a fire to cook the rice and squash they carried.

The cloth shelters and leafy lean-tos of the villagers dotted the mountainside and then disappeared as if an entire new village came to life each night and was destroyed in the morning when the march resumed. Sometimes the villagers smelled nerve gas wafting throughout the mountain ranges. They saw smoke rising from the distance, indicating burning villages. They feared the Pathet Lao, who were stalking them.

Finally they reached the Mekong. The men used their knives to cut down bamboo stalks and build makeshift rafts to hold their families. In desperation, some swam across the river. Babies strapped to their backs drowned as the weakened swimmers struggled. Others emptied water containers and tied them to their waists as flotation devices.

Escape

The flotilla of weary, pursued villagers made its way across the heavily guarded Mekong. They had escaped capture, torture, and killing by their enemies, the Pathet Lao. They were lucky. Many like them were tortured and killed or died of hunger in prison or en route.

When they landed in Thailand, the villagers were detained for two weeks in a temporary holding camp until moved to Ban Venai, one of the sixteen refugee camps in Thailand. The villagers from Joua Chang's village were relieved but exhausted and in some cases sick when they reached Thailand. As one man told an American journalist on the scene, "We [Hmong] . . . are all so tired. So many . . . are dead. We . . . people are so pitiful."

The Hmong villagers faced overcrowding and other poor conditions at the camp. They were offered little in the way of language or job training in preparation for a new home in a new culture. Medical care also was inadequate. Many at the camp suffered from malaria and dysentery. They shivered with fever. It was hard to tell the corpses from those still alive wrapped in black rags on dirty cots.

Those who were educated and who had served with the U.S. Special Forces in the war were given preferential treatment and priority for resettlement in the United States. But education was infrequent and negligible in Hmong villages, usually stopping at the third grade if it existed at all. And the practice of polygamy accepted by the Hmong—their practice was to take more than one wife—made many men unacceptable according to U.S. regulations.

Joua's service in the war and few years of school secured his family a place among those permitted early resettlement. After five months at the camp (many had to stay for years; even a year was considered a brief stay), they were sent by bus along the dusty road to Bangkok, twelve hours away. The bright lights of the city stunned the Changs' sleepy eyes. Her My and the children had never seen a city before, and the large buildings and neon signs startled and fascinated them. They clung tightly to Joua when they reached the airport as he stood in line with the other refugees to answer more questions. Before boarding a jet airliner to cross the Pacific, they were questioned and counted over and over until dawn.

After nearly boarding the wrong aircraft with another refugee contingent, the Changs were finally allowed to board the big jet that would take them the first leg of the trip to Wisconsin, with stops in Hong Kong, Tokyo, San Francisco, and Chicago.

In San Francisco, their first stop in the United States, they went through additional health, immigration, and customs checks. Then their flight to Chicago was followed by a long drive to the small town of Wausau, Wisconsin, with thirty-two thousand predominantly white "Middle Americans." Unlike Laos, snow covers the ground most of the winter in Wausau.

In Wausau the Changs were met by a Hmong woman working as a volunteer for Catholic Relief Services, a principal resettling agency for Indochinese. Members of their sponsoring church also were there to greet them, laden with warm coats and gloves for Joua and Her My, brightly colored snowsuits and boots for the three children.

The Changs' first days in their new town were as fraught with change as their trek from Laos the previous year had been. But there was help: The local church, Catholic Relief, state and federal authoritics, and the Hmong Mutual Assistance Association of Wisconsin all arranged for housing, employment counseling, job training, language classes, health care, and schooling. The U.S. government gave the new refugees five hundred dollars each to get started in America.

First Year of New Life

For most refugees the first year of the new life is taken up with basic issues of survival and adjustment. It was no different for the Changs. The sponsoring church had rented and painted a two-bedroom apartment for them. With its electric lights, refrigerator, and oven, it was a sharp contrast to their bamboo homes in the village in Laos. Despite the fact that many of their needs were taken care of, the first thing Joua Chang wanted for his family was "to stop being refugees." He wanted to find work to support them on his own. That meant he would have to improve his English.

The Hmong do not have as much trouble pronouncing English consonants as do other Indochinese refugee groups, since their seven-tone, monosyllabic language also involves a complicated coordination of mouth, lips, teeth, and throat. But they experience the same difficulties with tenses, irregular verbs, and plural forms. Joua knew a little English from his work with the

U.S. Special Forces. But all Her My could say so far was, "My name Her My. I'm fine, thank you." The children could say a little more, mostly words they had been taught to use in an emergency, such as "My name is ______. I'm lost."

Her My and Joua began to attend daily English classes with some of the other adult refugees in the area. The two boys, Vang and Chu, were enrolled in school and also in special English classes. Their quickness and enthusiasm for learning astounded their teachers. Youa, the baby, started going to a local day-care center.

Everyone was busy learning new words and new ways. Joua was learning how to drive. The Hmong woman who met them at the airport took Her My shopping at Wausau's largest supermarket, explaining what all the unfamiliar boxes and bottles were for and what they cost. Her My was surprised that bananas, so common in Laos, were so expensive in December in Wausau.

A Job

Two weeks after their arrival Joua had a job. A local furniture-making company hired him to do woodworking. He learned to operate the machinery quickly, and his dexterity and eagerness to succeed earned him a promotion after six months on the job. Her My began to work part-time as a grocery checkout clerk. She also sold her beautiful needlework in the intricately patterned Hmong style in a nearby crafts shop.

Eventually Joua and Her My became more fluent in English. Four years ago they started night school together to earn their high school diplomas. Now Joua is the bookkeeper for the same furniture company he started out with as a woodworker. He wants to begin an accounting course soon. Her My is a clerk-typist for a timber company in town.

The family was able to adapt well to its new life,

thanks to the help of the voluntary agencies who offered such necessities as training in English, job-finding assistance, and medical care. They were fortunate too that Joua and Her My stayed healthy and could lead the family in the strong Hmong family tradition. Many Hmong suffer from unexplained illnesses, and their death rate in the United States is high. Some attribute these deaths to the effects of the napalm they were heavily exposed to in Laos for so many years.

When they began to feel at home in Wausau, the Changs sent for Her My's sister and her family, who had escaped from Laos and were detained at another camp in Thailand. The two families hope to be able to pool their money and afford the down payment on a house in Wausau soon. Unlike some Indochinese refugees who leave their sponsoring towns for cities in states such as California where there are large communities of refugees like themselves, the Changs want to stay in Wausau. It was a long journey that brought them to Wisconsin, and as Her My says, "Everything is good for us here." Once again the Chang family are proud to call themselves Hmong, which means "free man." But now they are Americans as well. Now they are free people in a free country.

5

REFUGEES: SETTLING IN THE UNITED STATES

If the lamp pole had feet,
it would come here.

Vietnamese saying

The struggle to get to the United States was only the beginning. Many refugees found that settling here and finding out how to live new lives as independent citizens were far more difficult than their flights by land or boat. The story of the Vietnamese fisherfolk who settled on the Gulf Coast indicates some of the kinds of problems they experienced. During the resettlement efforts directed at placing the more than 120,000 Vietnamese refugees who arrived in this country in the spring of 1975, U.S. officials realized that many of the families from the coastal areas in the central and southern part of the country had made their livelihood as fisherfolk (a term used to include the women, whose contribution as netmakers and fishpackers was essential to the trade). These people were able to escape because they had access to boats on the coastal waters and were able to evacuate whole families on short notice. It is estimated that as much as one-third of Vietnam's fishing fleet departed in the exodus of the boat people.

Several seafood companies on the Florida Gulf Coast agreed to act as sponsors for some Vietnamese families and individuals with fishing experience because they needed workers as fishers and packers. Apart from their fishing experience, these refugees had few marketable skills; many were illiterate even in their own language, and three of the major companies started a program to train them in both basic English and American fishing techniques. Similar efforts were also underway in Louisiana and Texas.

A Fair Exchange

In the beginning these programs were considered fortunate arrangements for both parties—the companies who needed workers and who hoped the refugees would be skillful and work cheaply, and the Vietnamese, many of whom had been born on boats and had lived on them their whole lives, who would not have been skilled to do much else in our economy. But problems began to arise owing to culture and language misunderstandings and to the altered circumstances of the Vietnamese as refugees. For many of them this meant being reduced from prosperous, respected owners of their own businesses to working as deckhands for bosses whom they considered less knowledgeable than themselves. Some refugees felt that monies that had been paid to the companies by the volunteer resettlement agencies to offset the cost of training, housing, and other start-up expenses should have been paid directly to them. There was confusion about salary advances that were required to be paid back later. The refugees were the first to be laid off in slow times, and that seemed unfair to them. On the other hand, the companies felt that the refugees were taking advantage of them by learning the trade, the best places to fish, how the fish are marketed, and so forth.

In general, however, this resettlement sponsorship effort successfully introduced a significant number of refugees into a sector of the American economy. This success became evident as individual Vietnamese acquired boats of their own and went into business for themselves.

Very shortly after arriving, some Vietnamese began buying older small pleasure craft and outfitting them for fishing. Usually by pooling their money or by borrowing from friends, these entrepreneurs could begin fishing or shrimping using equipment that was secondhand or ingeniously improvised. Often family members would work in shifts around the clock. These businesses prospered when a second wave of immigrants came to the area from Vietnam, providing additional workers and enlarging the overall size of the foreign-born community in the area. Some were able to obtain loans for bigger boats and hire their countrymen as employees. In 1980 more than sixty fishing boats owned by Vietnamese worked the Gulf waters off western Florida's coast. But in order for these refugees to succeed, many obstacles had to be overcome.

"Rules of the Road"

As immigrants the fisherfolk were forbidden to go farther than three miles from the coast. This restriction limited them to densely fished waters. In Vietnam almost no regulations had restricted their fishing activity, but here they faced confusing federal, state, city, and county rules. Often they were aware of a rule only after they had broken it. Many of their infractions involved violations of safety regulations, such as requirements for fire extinguishers, life preservers, safe containers for fuel, proper placement of running lights, knowledge of and adherence to the "rules of the road" for passing other ships, and so on.

Many of the difficulties the fisherfolk encountered were the result of cultural differences. For example, certain seabirds such as pelicans, which are protected by federal law in the United States, are commonly eaten in Vietnam. For Americans to see the Vietnamese openly catching and dressing the birds to be eaten caused them to view the newcomers not only as lawbreakers but as strange as well. Similarly, the taking of undersized shrimp, which is illegal, was routinely practiced by the Vietnamese. They did not necessarily intend to sell them for profit but instead wanted to eat them as a staple of their diet, but this illegal practice also caused friction between the two groups.

Another cultural difference that caused continuous strain involved the boat-handling methods of the two groups. Many Vietnamese did not observe the American expectations with regard to waiting their turn when lining up for fuel or for unloading the day's catch, and instead they cut ahead of other boats. The locals were upset with the seemingly haphazard approach the refugees took to allowing sufficient space for safe passage between boats underway on the high seas. The refugees were also indifferent to less formal but nevertheless long-standing agreements about who has priority to fish in various areas for certain periods of time. The standard practice of following an agreed-on pattern when trawling was also ignored. The Vietnamese seemed to use no particular pattern to charge in and out among other trawling boats. Also it was considered unacceptably bad manners when the Vietnamese barged into an area where someone else had begun to make a good catch without being invited by radio contact.

Americans were greatly irritated by the Vietnamese's very casual attitude toward contact between boats. Most of the Vietnamese boats were secondhand and being worked very hard with no expectation that they would last very long and with no value at all given to their appearance. In Vietnam boats were replaced every few years and were considered to be somewhat disposable. So, understandably, the fisherfolk could afford to be fairly careless about bumping and other unnecessary contact between boats when mooring or otherwise maneuvering. In sharp contrast to this style was the Americans' attitude, which considers it a mark of bad seamanship, reflecting on the owners' standing in the community, to have a boat that was scratched or dented.

In addition to the overzealous fishing patterns, the Vietnamese practiced very intensive methods of fishing, such as rotating crews to work a boat around the clock. They also were more accustomed to fishing in bad weather or when the catch was so poor it barely justified the cost of going to sea. These efforts, which contributed so much to the Vietnamese's success, were resented by the Americans, who felt that their livelihood was being threatened.

Probably the single most troublesome conflict resulted from the kind of nets that the Vietnamese commonly used. Conventionally, the Gulf area fishermen use nets that are shorter than two thousand feet, and they are set and picked up at frequent intervals. Not only did the Vietnamese use nets up to five thousand feet in length, but they would set them end to end, entirely covering a large area, and furthermore they would leave them in place overnight. The Americans bitterly opposed this technique. They felt that the Vietnamese practices monopolized too large an area for too long a time in a business that was dependent on the unpredictable movements of schools of fish from hour to hour.

Two counties of Florida passed a law outlawing the use of gill nets longer than two thousand feet. The Vietnamese tried to contest the law but finally had to shorten their nets, and because of the lost productivity, some were forced to shift to shrimping.

Generally, these conflicts were mediated by the volunteers working for the resettlement agencies. In cooperation with local authorities and law enforcement officials, they instructed the Vietnamese concerning the customs, laws, and regulations pertaining to commercial fishing in the United States. Translators and counselors for offenders going to court proceedings were made available, and assistance was given to help the Vietnamese bring their boats up to the required safety standards. Social service workers also tried to educate the community and the American fishermen to the reality of the new immigrants' intentions and experiences.

More Benefit than Hurt

The experiences of the Vietnamese fisherfolk in the seafood industry of the Florida, Louisiana, and Texas Gulf coasts demonstrate some of the difficulties that arise when ethnic groups with widely different cultural backgrounds are thrown together in competition for jobs, housing, and the right to maintain and to express their own cultural identities. Inevitably some Americans retaliated vindictively against the Vietnamese. But on the whole there is no doubt that more have benefited from the Vietnamese's productivity than have been hurt, including packers and processors who have marketed the Vietnamese's catch and consumers who have had more fish and seafood available.

In the next chapter we look at why and how refugees from Cuba, Central America, and the Caribbean, as well as the Soviet Union, have come to our country, and at some of the cultural conflicts they have experienced during their transition to becoming new Americans.

6

REFUGEES: CUBANS, CENTRAL AMERICANS, HAITIANS, AND SOVIETS

You can be born here in a Cuban hospital, be baptized by a Cuban priest, buy all your food from a Cuban grocer, take your insurance from a Cuban Bank . . . .

Maurice Ferre
Mayor of Miami

One of the most difficult and controversial crises in U.S. immigration history began in early April 1980 and reads like a spy-thriller novel by Graham Greene. There were hints that a Soviet master spy was helping Cuba's premier, Fidel Castro, to orchestrate a propaganda coup by permitting a handful of Cubans who had taken refuge inside the Peruvian embassy in Havana to leave the country. Normally, Cubans are not permitted to emigrate from their country, and Castro has been at odds with South American countries who have helped Cubans to escape. Washington intelligence sources reported that former Soviet spy Kim Philby was seen in Havana and may have been behind Castro's removing the guards from around the Peruvian embassy and dismissing the dissidents hiding inside as nothing but "common delinquents, anti-socials, vagrants, and bums."

Cuba was not prepared, however, for what followed. For years Cuba has been plagued with high unemployment and widespread corruption. So when Castro announced that the Cubans hiding in the Peruvian embassy were free to leave, other dissatisfied Cubans flocked to the embassy seeking sanctuary also. Within two days more than ten thousand refugees were cramped onto the grounds—sleeping on the grass, in the trees, even on the embassy roof. Some would wait for up to two weeks for rescue, some without food for the last five to seven days. One person later described the scene: "There were the crowds outside shouting and screaming at us. They called us traitors and deserters. Many of my friends came to the embassy to seek refuge and get out of Cuba, but they were too late and couldn't get in. There is no liberty in Cuba. None." The large and well-established Cuban community in Miami, many of whose members have prospered since fleeing Castro's revolution twenty years before, responded with efforts to rescue their fellow countrymen, many of them relatives. For example, *Newsweek* reported the case of the *Viking Starship*, a 140-foot fishing boat that was chartered by a group of Cuban-Americans to sail to Mariel Harbor in Cuba to pick up a group of their relatives. But after the embarrassing debacle of the Peruvian embassy incident, Castro had decided to take advantage of the situation and had announced that all who wanted to leave Cuba could do so. When the *Viking Starship* arrived in Mariel, however, it was detained for nearly a week, and was then allowed to leave only if it took almost five hundred refugees chosen by Castro. None of the seventy-five relatives of the group who had chartered the boat were among them. According to members of the crew, "We had to take what the Cuban government wanted us to take. . . . Few boats are getting any relatives out. I didn't see anybody hugging and kissing at Mariel."

In the next two weeks almost nineteen thousand Cubans were carried to Florida by a huge flotilla of boats in what became known as the Mariel boatlift. This was twice the number the United States had said it would accept. What was worse, according to Representative Elizabeth Holtzman (D-NY), then head of the House Subcommittee on Immigration, Refugees, and International Law, as many as seven hundred of the arrivals were ex-convicts who had been rounded up by the Cuban government and given the choice of going to America or going back to jail. Meanwhile would-be refugees seeking visas at the American diplomatic offices were attacked by Cuban government security guards with clubs. Many fought back with bricks and many were wounded; 389 persons sought asylum in the U.S. office. Others in Cuba had to wait for days just for the use of a telephone to call someone in Florida, hoping to arrange to be picked up. Thousands waited on the beach at Mariel, twenty miles west of Havana, for a place on the "freedom flotilla" that was coming. Not since the British evacuated the beaches at Dunkirk during World War II with a similar "mini-armada" had a sea-rescue mission been undertaken by such a motley collection of small craft, including motorboats, commercial shrimpers, even the former presidential yacht *Sequoia.*

"An Open Heart"

At first the official U.S. response was very cautious. The U.S. economy had its own unemployment problems, and according to a State Department spokesman, "There is no way that the U.S. can accommodate a mass influx of immigrants at this time." President Carter had at first threatened to impound the boats that were transporting Cubans and heavily fine their owners. But the administration's resentment at Castro for trying to dump his problems at our doorstep soon gave way to humanitarian concern for the refugees. It was clear that Miami's Cubans would not in any case give up their sealift efforts, and the prospect of another tragedy like that of the Southeast Asian boat people prompted the United States to attempt to make accommodations for at least some of the refugees. President Carter declared, "We'll continue to provide an open heart and open our minds to refugees seeking freedom from Communist domination and from the economic deprivation brought about by Fidel Castro and his government."

Solving the problems involved in this sudden mass immigration required more than the best of intentions, however. By the fourth week more than thirty thousand refugees had landed in Florida, and the question began to be asked: Were there practical limits to the number that the United States could ultimately admit?

Improvised Facilities

The federal government opened a processing center and temporary shelter at Florida's Eglin Air Force base, once the site of resettlement for Indochinese refugees. More than 150 tents were set up, each sheltering thirty individuals in a space eighteen by fifty-two feet square; aircraft hangars were jammed with rows of cots; dormitories and gymnasiums were filled; forest area was cleared to make room for temporary shelter. Thousands more found refuge in the corridors of the Orange Bowl in Miami, and in other smaller shelters across the Florida Panhandle. President Carter released ten million dollars in funds for refugee emergency relief to cover the cost of feeding, transporting, and processing the Cubans. Five hundred U.S. Marines were sent to relieve the Florida National Guardsmen at camps in Key West, the major point of arrival. And Fort Chaffee in Arkansas was opened to accommodate twenty thousand refugees awaiting resettlement. The government flew in five hundred tons of food, a mobile hospital, and portable showers.

All this activity was largely improvised, because the United States had no coherent policy or plans for handling this number of refugees this rapidly. The process quickly bogged down and backed up as more Cubans kept arriving. On one day, forty-five hundred Cubans arrived, more than had arrived in over one month after the revolution in the early 1960s. In three weeks the total was more than double the number of Indochinese refugees arriving in a month the previous year.

From their landing sites in the Florida Keys and along the coast the arriving refugees were first bused to Key West Naval Air Station, where up to five thousand waited at a time in hot and crowded quarters. Officials of the U.S. Immigration and Naturalization Service checked in the new arrivals, who were then served juice and sandwiches in a makeshift cafeteria before being boarded on buses and taken to their processing center. The largest of these centers was at Tamiami Park outside Miami. There an average of fifteen hundred refugees a day were led through a seven-step process leading to their release to join relatives or to be resettled at temporary sites. Often amid much confusion, the tired and nervous Cubans were led to waiting areas and given name tags and numbers as well as medical attention. Fights broke out as tempers flared when some refugees claimed they had spotted Castro spies in their midst. After the long and arduous journey the patience of many refugees broke during the final hours' wait to board the buses or to gain their clearances.

Arriving Cubans were told that if they had relatives beyond Miami, they would be given plane tickets to join them. Others would be permitted to live and work where they wished, after being released from temporary shelters and processing centers. A coalition of Cuban exile groups called the Cuban Patriotic Junta gave forty dollars cash to each newcomer.

The new arrivals were declared eligible for food stamps and received forms for them. They received work permits and Social Security cards. Initially, they were considered undocumented aliens seeking asylum and were not eligible for medical care paid for by the government, aid to dependent children, or cash assistance.

Miami New Home for Most

The city of Miami, with the largest Cuban-American population in the United States, had become the settling place of choice of the majority of the refugees. The first mass exodus of Cubans had occurred in 1961 following Castro's revolution, and more than five hundred thousand Cuban Americans have established themselves there in the twenty years since. In the process they have transformed the glamorous resort city into a center for Latin American commercial investment and international banking. But there were signs that any further Latinization would strain the city beyond its ability to function. The new Cubans arrived at a time when jobs and housing were becoming increasingly scarce.

The attraction of Miami for the latest exiles is

understandable. In 1960 the percentage of non-Latin whites in Miami's Dade County was 80 percent; in 1980, before the boatlift, it was 45 percent. Miami had become a bilingual, bicultural city where it is very easy for Cubans to get along without ever learning English; indeed, often it is the English-only-speaking population that is more hampered. Job applicants are often required to speak Spanish, and it can be difficult to find clerks in stores, for example, who speak English. Signs saying "English spoken here" are not uncommon. Many businesses are owned by Cubans, and an estimated two hundred former Cuban exiles are millionaires today. In some neighborhoods Cuban cultural traditions are so predominant that a casual stroller would think he or she was in Havana.

"Pull up the Gangplank"

This accommodation to Hispanic culture did not occur without causing a backlash among other segments of Miami's population. With the new inundation of Cubans, many non-Latins felt that the city had gone overboard in aiding the refugees, that the city was being taken away from them. Many non-Latins moved away; many others adopted an attitude that was called a gangplank mentality—that is, "Now we're all aboard, let's pull up the gangplank and keep the rest out." This opposition sentiment called for closing the borders completely to refugees and all illegal aliens.

Some of the fears centered on widespread rumors that Castro was emptying his jails and sending many hard-core criminals to the United States. But although there were some ex-convicts and thugs among the refugees, most were political prisoners, not common lawbreakers. Immigration and Naturalization Service (INS) officials were unable to discriminate accurately among all the refugees, even when fellow refugees or Miami police thought they had detected known felons, because they had no way of checking out their stories. In any case, those suspected could not be sent back to Cuba because Castro refused to accept any returnees. Several hundred suspected criminals were sent to the federal correctional institution in Talladega, Alabama, for further screening.

Other concerns for the Miami community were the scarcity of housing and jobs. For the refugees it was a problem not just to find decent housing but to find anything at all. The vacancy rate for private apartments was extremely low, and the rents were too high in any case for refugees earning minimum wages or less. In some cases the newcomers were forced to sleep in abandoned buildings or to crowd into the apartments of friends and relatives, sometimes sleeping in shifts. In the job market most were forced to compete for the few menial jobs available, with employers taking advantage of the situation by offering far less than minimum wage.

Clear, and to some, troublesome, differences distinguished the latest Cuban refugees from those who preceded them. Between 1959 and 1962 the first wave of two hundred thousand came from Cuba in an organized airlift. Most of them had been prosperous under the system before Castro's revolution. More than 90 percent were white, middle-aged, and well educated. The majority came with their families, and they have done well in this country. From 1965 to 1970, 270,000 Cubans came. In this group almost 25 percent were black or mulatto. They were mostly educated tradesmen from Cuba's working class, and they also brought their families. In 1980 the vast majority of "Marielitos" had much less education; some were blue-collar workers. Many of the men had not been allowed to bring their families. This group had a much higher divorce rate; twenty thousand of the men (who were much younger than those of the first two groups) were separated from their wives. About half of them were black, and most spoke only Spanish.

Despite all the obstacles, of the more than 120,000

Cubans who had arrived in the boatlift, nearly 110,000 of them had been resettled by the year's end, more than 70,000 in the Miami area. Approximately 12,000 were still in four refugee camps, at Fort Chaffee in Arkansas, Fort McCoy in Wisconsin, Fort Indiantown Gap in Pennsylvania, and Eglin Air Force Base in Florida. The majority of these were single, uneducated men with no job skills and no friends or relatives. It was costing the government an estimated one million dollars a week to run these camps and centers.

On the positive side, considering the predictions of disaster that had accompanied the refugees' arrival and in the face of nearly insurmountable difficulties, most of the Marielitos are at least holding their own today, and some have been successful. An article from the *New York Times* reprinted in the Lutheran Immigration and Refugee Service Bulletin gave the following individuals as examples of those who have conquered the challenge: Eduardo Suarez, a photographer who worked for a television station in Miami and won an Emmy for his news coverage, and Jesus Sarmiento, who graduated from Florida International University with an engineering degree and a 3.5 grade average, the first Marielito to become a college graduate in this country.

The director of the Miami International Rescue Committee, Cecil Gaudie, estimates that better than 85 percent of the Mariel refugees have jobs and are self-supporting. Judge Seymour Gelber, the administrator of the Dade County juvenile court, has indicated that the predicted rise in juvenile crime among Hispanic children has not occurred to the degree expected.

El Salvador's Innocent Citizens

Cuba's citizens are not the only Latins seeking new lives in this country. Many others from Central and South American and Caribbean nations have fled the poverty and political and social turmoil of their homelands for the United States. For example, it is estimated that a few hundred thousand men and women have fled the small Central American country of El Salvador for the United States, fugitives from the ravages of a civil war and the accompanying upheaval. The Foreign Affairs Committee of the U.S. House of Representatives has reported that fighting in El Salvador between leftist guerrillas and U.S.-backed government troops threatens the lives of many of the country's "innocent citizens." The committee also has recommended that refugees from that country should be given temporary asylum here until they can safely return. Despite this recommendation, the Reagan administration claims that the fugitives should be sent back to their homeland because they have entered the United States illegally.

In one recent year the State Department ordered over five thousand Salvadorans back to the tiny, war-torn nation. Many are reported to have been killed on their return. According to Amnesty International and the Catholic Archdiocese of San Salvador, in 1980, 30 percent of all returning deportees from the United States never made it back to their communities. They "disappeared," a synonym for "dead" in El Salvador parlance. Santana Rivera, a twenty-one-year-old illegal immigrant taken in by a church group in Seattle, tells a story of violent reprisals against those suspected of sympathizing with or helping the various guerrillas who desire to overthrow the Salvadoran government: "The army burned our homes and towns. . . . They went on killing sprees, massacring women, children, old people. One day my father and two uncles were captured and killed by National Guardsmen on their way home from work. They brought my father's head to my mother to show her what might happen to us."

After his village was burned, Santana's mother took the family to the capital, San Salvador. Santana tried to find work to support her and the twelve other children. There was no work for him. After deciding to leave his country to find work in the United States to support his mother and brothers and sisters, he fled via the illegal route through Mexico to Los Angeles. From there he traveled with migrant fruit pickers to Oregon and then to Washington.

Many Salvadorans have been apprehended working in the fertile farmland and orchards of Washington in raids by the INS. Santana was arrested for driving without a license in rural Washington and was put in the Renton city jail, where the INS in that area detains illegal aliens. He stayed there for a month until a Quaker church group posted bond for his release. He now lives with a Quaker family, who also house another Salvadoran and a Guatemalan, all of whom hope to petition the government for refugee status, a long, difficult, discouraging process.

The Reagan administration maintains that most Salvadorans here are not escaping indiscriminate political violence in their country but are seeking a better economic situation. U.S. law limiting asylum to refugees who can show "a well-founded fear" that they would be in danger if they returned home necessitates that each Salvadoran show evidence and prove his or her case. In 1982, 14,078 Salvadorans were caught by the INS; 4,873 were deported. Only 74 out of 1,141 who applied for asylum were accepted. Today thousands more applications are pending; meanwhile others hide from the authorities and hope for a change in the law.

In the Seattle area many churches and individuals like the Quaker family helping Santana have come to the aid of the immigrants. Citing a Christian tradition of harboring the needy and homeless and of fostering peace and unity, they give sanctuary to thousands of illegals, defying what they believe to be an immoral practice by our government. A group of lawyers also works for the refugees' legal acceptance. One attorney from the group said he feels that the United States should authorize "extended voluntary departure" status for the Salvadorans, permitting them to stay here until the fighting in their homeland ends, a practice used in the past with other refugee groups.

While they either wait for deportation or work for legalization of their status, many Salvadorans in the state of Washington continue to be harbored by church members and groups, sometimes illegally. Immigration officials claim that church workers are attracting more refugees to the state, which probably is home to nearly four thousand Salvadorans who are in the United States illegally.

The local INS director feels that the church members are "well-intentioned" but in some cases could be breaking the law, for instance, if they told an INS officer with a search warrant that no one was living in their home when actually an illegal immigrant was there or if they helped smuggle aliens along a secret route and into church sanctuaries. Yet the number of those aiding the Salvadorans is increasing. And many are safe—for now.

Last year seven illegal Salvadoran refugees were bailed out of jail by fourteen thousand dollars donated by members of Seattle churches. As the Reverend Donovan Cook, pastor of one of the churches, said, the donation was "an expression of the religious sensitivity and compassion of the people." One of the larger contributions was two thousand dollars from a deacon in Mr. Cook's church, who put his house up for a promissory note to free Oscar Cruz, a former Salvadoran student arrested at a Washington fruit orchard. "I just didn't want to see him sent back and killed," the deacon said. Twenty-eight-year-old Cruz, who is fluent in English, was overwhelmed by the generosity of the church people: "Our lives have been at risk," he said. "The students were denouncing the government's injustices. That put us in great danger."

Cruz wants to see his country united again and the people righting the widespread injustices through economic and social reform. He would like to go back and help his people, but he believes he would surely be met with death.

Supporters of temporary asylum for the Salvadorans have called their transport home "death flights." In Congress, Representative Romano Mazzoli asked why temporary asylum was granted to Chileans and Ethiopians when civil war threatened their citizens but denied Salvadorans. "Why is there a distinction for El Salvador?" he asked. Some say the reason for the distinction lies in U.S. support of the El Salvador government. They conjecture that granting asylum to the Salvadorans would in effect admit to the injustices and violent methods of that government reported by the fugitives.

Haitians—A Special Case

"Dying of hunger and being executed by the government are the same thing." This statement by Haitian priest Father Rollin Darbouze in Brooklyn, New York, points up the dilemma of the United States when faced with the situation in Haiti and how to deal with the Haitians here illegally who petition for refugee status.

The *World Refugee Survey 1983* reported that eight hundred thousand Haitians left their country in search of greater economic opportunity in the previous fifteen years. Haiti's "president for life" Jean-Claude Duvalier, "Baby Doc," is said to have improved the economic situation since the death of his father, "Papa Doc," but in actuality he has done little. Many poverty-stricken Haitians have fled to the United States, even though the Haitian government and our government have agreed to restrict this flow. In fact, Haiti's government is the only one in the Caribbean (other than Cuba) that makes it difficult for residents to leave, even on tourist visas.

Those Haitians who fled to Florida in 1980, taking advantage of the Cuban situation in the hope that they too would be admitted, arrived in their boats at the same time as the Cuban "Marielitos" released by Castro. Their timing was good, and they were lucky. Since the U.S. government would have to face a difficult and embarrassing situation if they turned back the black Haitians and not the mostly white Cubans, the fifteen thousand Haitians were given the same special "parole," admitting them as "special entrants," as were the Cubans. One refugee coordinator said, "Let's be realistic. You don't push back the boats. The great majority of these people are going to stay here."

But after their arrival, the Haitians have had to fight for acceptance. The U.S. position is that these Haitians must *prove* racial, political, or religious persecution and that they have not come here to escape poverty. Since 80 percent of the Haitian population live on less than $150 a year, the poverty line in that country's economy, Haitians in the United States are certainly economic refugees. But are they also acceptable under the terms of our refugee policy as set forth by the Refugee Act of 1980? The distinction is a difficult one.

Sorting out legitimate political refugees from the many who seek relief from extreme poverty is an emotionally stressful dilemma. "Once you say 'economic refugee,' you've got the whole world," one planner said. A White House aide commented, "These people are the tip of an enormous number who want to come to the United States for a better life."

Like those fleeing El Salvador and seeking refugee status here, Haitians fear that deportation would mean death on arrival back in Haiti. And one need not be an opponent of the Duvalier government, they say. As Father Darbouze said, "You never know if you're involved in Haitian politics or not"—until you are sent back and step off the plane in Haiti, never to be heard of again. The consensus is that all Haitians are seen as being either for Duvalier or against him. To be against him may mean death.

Soviet Jewish Refugees— High Expectations

Part of that "enormous number" who want to come to the United States for a better life are the Soviet Jewish refugees. From 1969 to 1980 about seventy thousand Russian Jews came to the United States; almost half came in 1979 alone. Since 1980 the flow has been lighter because the Soviet government has permitted fewer to leave. Although their numbers are not so great as the Hispanics and Asians, their case is compelling. Not only do they suffer in their homeland from economic, social, and, of course, political repression, they are denied the right to practice their religion freely.

Jews in the Soviet Union face discrimination in access to education and in acceptance for employment, as well as difficulty finding advancement opportunities in jobs. When they have been able to afford to come here, most have been permitted to leave if they can prove they intend to join their families. But sometimes the process is long and problematic. Some have been forced to leave under false pretenses and then seek asylum in the United States when using travel or study visas. When they do arrive, however, they have come with the tools that would seem to give them a better chance of success than most. They are usually skilled in a profession or trade. A support network of other Jews is ready to assist them with housing and employment.

But along with other refugees, Soviet Jews share a lack of understanding about life and opportunities in the

United States. Their expectations are mismatched to present-day realities. As one staffer at the Hebrew Immigrants Aid Society said, "They hear it's so good here. They think they're falling into a honey nest." The Council of Jewish Federation reported in 1979 that "Soviet Jews arriving in this country are a strongly motivated, determined and work-conscious population with high, demanding (if not unrealistic at times) expectations for the labor market and their appropriate place in it. . . . That these expectations cannot always be fulfilled is due to a number of problems." "They think we can open all the doors for them," added an official of the New York Association for New Americans. "It's a cultural conflict from the day they land."

Eventually most of the Russians do find work. But it is not always what they expected. Life in Russia gave them little preparation for the U.S. job market and its tradition of upward mobility for those who start at the bottom. Stories of U.S. wealth led them to dream of a different America from the one where they may be forced to drive a cab or do manual labor even though they have advanced degrees or technical experience. It is difficult for them to grasp the idea that here you can build a career from the bottom rung up and that one job leads to a better one. As with all refugees, life in a new country brings a new set of problems and ways to master them.

Certainly our refugee policy has been one that has shown compassion toward those who have proved their case of persecution according to the terms of the Refugee Act of 1980. But is that sufficient? What about the fate of those like the Haitians and the others whose governments are not condemned and repudiated officially by the United States? Some argue that we do not accept some of those who are greatly in need. Many of those we deny admission may be imprisoned or killed in their countries. And some, denied legal admission, will attempt to enter the United States illegally. Here they join the millions of illegal, deportable aliens who have fled from poverty or religious and social persecution or political repression. For whatever reason, they have been unable to prove why they should stay here legally. Their stories are told in the next chapter.

7

ILLEGAL IMMIGRANTS AND OUR BORDERS

Everywhere around the world,
They're coming to America!

Neil Diamond
"America"

The majority of illegal aliens, sometimes called undocumented workers, are persons of foreign origin who have entered the country unlawfully, bypassing inspection. A much smaller number of people become illegal aliens after having entered the country legally and then violating the terms of their stay, usually by overstaying and/or accepting employment.

Because undocumented workers are seeking to remain undiscovered, it is difficult to gather information about them. The best estimates suggest that there are approximately four million to six million aliens in the United States today who have not been admitted legally or who have overstayed legal admission terms and have accepted employment illegally, with more than a million entering each year. In 1983 the Immigration and Naturalization Service located more than 1,220,000 of these deportable aliens (up from only 86,000 apprehensions in 1964).

Today the number of people entering the United States illegally is more than double the number who enter legally. A large number of those apprehended are believed to be repeat offenders, coming and going almost at will, for stays of varying lengths. An estimated 50 to 60 percent of all illegal aliens are Mexican.

Looking for Work

Most illegal immigrants are influenced by political, economic, and social forces in the home nations that push them to seek homes and employment in our country, known throughout the world as the "land of opportunity." Certainly the chief inducement is the search for employment at better wages. The principal sources of illegal entrants to the United States are the nearby developing countries, Mexico and those of the Caribbean basin, where unemployment is high and wages low. In addition to ease of access and better economic prospects, other factors contributing to illegal immigration are the lack of effective enforcement of our immigration laws and the existence in the United States of communities of fellow countrymen who can offer support and assistance.

Employers in this country in certain industries, particularly agriculture, restaurant/hotel work, and the garment and service industries, have been willing to hire undocumented workers in spite of their illegal status. Indeed, aliens are sought out because they are often willing to work for lower wages than are citizen workers. Because the lowest U.S. wages are so much higher than what they can get at home and because they fear being detected, they are easily exploited by those who offer substandard wages and working conditions. In areas where illegal aliens are available fairly constantly or periodically, as during the harvesting season, their presence is believed to depress the wages of citizen workers and to frustrate the effective organization of workers. For example, at some automobile plants in southern California, assembly line workers, as many as half of whom are illegal aliens, earn about two dollars less than assembly line workers in northern California plants, where there are few illegal workers. But not all undocumented workers do menial or low-paying work. The INS has apprehended illegal aliens who were working at plastics and electronic companies, construction jobs, foundries, meat-packing plants, snack food producers, and other jobs where the pay is higher and the working conditions better than in unskilled labor jobs.

The Reagan administration's Interagency Task Force on Immigration estimates that five hundred thousand *permanent* illegal aliens per year are added to the population. If this is correct, then they are taking more than

25 percent of all new jobs created each year. Ray Marshall, a former Secretary of Labor, concludes that even if only two million of the four to six million illegal aliens in the country at any given time are holding jobs that could be held by citizens, eliminating this displacement would bring the country up to the standard of full employment.

Most observers believe that the real economic impact of immigrant labor, legal and illegal alike, is felt most by those least able to bear it—black teenagers and working-class heads of households. Young unskilled blacks who are fighting for entry-level positions in the work force find that they are, in effect, competing for these jobs against the world's poor who have come here seeking a better life. Unionized labor believes that illegals put unfair pressure on the working person to accept wages and conditions the unions have been struggling for decades to improve. An undocumented worker who cannot risk being discovered will accept pay and conditions that no one should have to accept. It does seem to be true that illegals hold some jobs that are considered too dirty, too back-breaking, too wretched for the meager pay for anyone else to want.

Two Strategies for Coping

Several measures can be adopted to help curtail illegal immigration. The first is to improve the enforcement of our present immigration policy. No one disagrees that illegal entry to and residence in the United States are entirely too easy for illegal aliens to achieve. It is doubtful that any level of enforcement could completely eliminate illegal entry, given the force of the pressures to emigrate. But it could be significantly improved. At present there are fewer than 3,000 Border Patrol officials; at any one time fewer than 500 are available to patrol the entire 2,000 miles of unfortified border with Mexico, where the vast majority of illegals enter the country. Fewer than 25 percent of deportable aliens located in the interior of the country are apprehended.

The second measure to restrict illegal immigration is to adopt a new immigration policy. This is the intention of the legislation known as the Simpson-Mazzoli bill.

Simpson-Mazzoli Bill

The dramatic increase in illegal immigration over the last decade is really the impetus for various reforms demanded by both ordinary citizens and high government officials. Employment of illegal aliens and how to control it are at the heart of a landmark piece of legislation that attempts the most drastic reform of our nation's immigration policy in a generation or more—the Simpson-Mazzoli bill.

Former U.S. attorney general, William French Smith, issued a statement in October 1983 that summarized the need for legislation like that proposed by Senator Alan Simpson (R-Wy) and Congressman Romano Mazzoli (D-Ky):

> The issues concerning immigration reform are among the most important facing this nation today. . . .

- We have lost control of our borders
- illegal immigration is massive and growing
- vast numbers of jobs that could be held by Americans are taken by illegal aliens
- illegal aliens constitute an enormous drain on our social and welfare services
- illegal immigration makes a mockery of our legal immigration system

- millions of illegal aliens—most of whom are Hispanic—have become an exploited class preyed upon by the unscrupulous.

The debate in the Senate and the House over Simpson-Mazzoli was long, bitter and full of conflict. In President Reagan's words, the main intent of the legislation was to regain "control of our own borders," and to bring the shadow society of illegal aliens into the light so that it can be given both the rights and the duties of our legal system. Versions of the bill were passed by the Senate in May 1983 and by the House in July 1984. At the heart of both the House and the Senate versions are two major reform measures, employer sanctions and amnesty.

The most controversial issue concerning immigration and the current legislation is the proposed use of employer sanctions, or penalties on employers who hire illegal aliens, as a means of controlling illegal immigration and undocumented workers in the United States. If the prospect of gaining employment at U.S. wages is the magnet drawing aliens here illegally, an effective deterrent might be to penalize employers who knowingly hire illegal aliens. By making it illegal to employ them, we eliminate work opportunities and remove the attraction for coming here. (Under present laws it is generally not illegal to hire undocumented workers, although, if caught, the workers may be deported.) House proponents of employer sanctions passed the part of the Simpson-Mazzoli bill that would fine employers up to two thousand dollars for hiring undocumented workers on June 13, 1984, but they failed to impose the suggested prison terms.

Hispanic organizations are firmly opposed to these employer sanctions. They believe that a crackdown on employers would tend to make them suspicious of anyone with a Hispanic surname or even a different appearance. Fearing that by hiring such a person they might be hiring an undocumented worker who will get them into trouble, employers would tend to discriminate against all Hispanics as a group. And employers who are biased to begin with would have a convenient excuse to avoid hiring Hispanics.

Proponents of sanctions maintain that some form of identification could avert such discrimination. All employers would be required to examine specific documentation from job applicants, with penalties for failure to do so. A signed affidavit from both the employer and the new person hired would be the employer's proof that he or she had complied with the law.

The problem with this proposal is the concept of a "national identity card" to be used as proof of eligibility to work. The American Civil Liberties Union and other civil rights advocates believe that this might be the basis for a national data bank that would be an infringement on individual rights to privacy. Any legislation of sanctions would have to implement a forge-proof, verifiable card or other system that would be an acceptable proof of identity.

The American Federation of Labor–Congress of Industrial Organizations (AFL-CIO) strongly endorses employer sanctions because they believe that illegal aliens are taking jobs away from American workers and that the sanction would discourage such illegals from coming to the United States in search of such work. Not everyone agrees that this is so. Hispanic groups argue that ridding the work place of undocumented workers would not result in many more jobs becoming available to American workers.

Amnesty

Closely associated with efforts to stem the tide of illegal aliens is the proposal, also part of the Simpson-Mazzoli bill, to grant amnesty to those who are already here. This legalization of their status is supported on the grounds of equity and the lack of any viable alternative. Many undocumented workers are productive members of society. The United States bears some responsibility for their presence here, since our immigration policy has been ambivalent, holding out the prospect of jobs to some and not enforcing the border restrictions. The only alternative to amnesty is the unsavory prospect of mass roundups and deportations. This was tried once in 1954 in the program referred to as Operation Wetback. Not only not feasible in terms of money and manpower, it is a degrading and inhuman process that would not be tolerated today.

Various provisions under consideration call for residency requirements of varying lengths to qualify for amnesty. For example, the Simpson-Mazzoli bill calls for a two-tier requirement. Aliens who are otherwise eligible who have been here since January 1, 1977, would immediately qualify for permanent-resident status. Those who had entered prior to January 1, 1980 (or January 1, 1982, according to the House version of the bill), would qualify for temporary status and would convert to permanent status in two years if they could demonstrate competency in English.

Such legislation is not acceptable to some critics because they believe that it condones and encourages law breaking. Some city, county, and state governments are concerned about the economic effects on public assistance programs of newly eligible legalized aliens. They want the federal government to pick up the costs.

Even some Hispanic groups have reservations about the form amnesty would take. While most consider it to be a step in the right direction, they fear that many aliens who come forward to apply for amnesty would be excluded on other grounds and deported. Some think that most illegal aliens would not come forward because of this fear. The uncertain status of temporary-resident aliens offered to the arrivals after 1980 is unacceptable to them because it would create a "subclass" of workers denied some rights of full citizenship. Therefore, Hispanics are pressing for reliable and certain status for those illegal aliens willing to step forward and apply for amnesty.

Guest Workers

The desire to gain control of our borders and curtail illegal entry to the United States is complicated by the fact that undeniably many undocumented workers are significant components in certain industries. It is likely that there will always be a need for workers on a temporary, usually seasonal, basis—in agriculture, for example.

Organized labor opposes guest-worker programs for the same reason it opposes illegal immigrants—that the importation of foreign workers in any manner undercuts U.S. wages and working conditions.

The Select Committee on Immigration and Refugee Policy, which included former presidents Jimmy Carter and Gerald Ford as well as such notables as Reverend Theodore Hesburgh, president of Notre Dame University, and Barbara Jordan, former congresswoman and a professor at the University of Texas, rejected any large-scale temporary guest-worker program when they completed their study of the issues. The Reagan administration had proposed a two-year experimental program of fifty thousand Mexican workers annually but later dropped it in favor of modifications of the existing program. Such modifications are a part of the House version of the Simpson-Mazzoli bill. They would make it relatively easy for employers to qualify for hiring seasonal farm workers.

Although the controversy over Simpson-Mazzoli and the measures it proposed will no doubt continue into the next decade and beyond, most people throughout the country feel that any solution is better than no solution to the problems of illegal immigration. As *Newsweek* magazine reported in June 1984, "The real argument for Simpson-Mazzoli is that there is probably no better way to clean up the mess—and that it is time to do *something*."

The mess *Newsweek* referred to is nowhere more apparent than at the border. Corruption, violence, and widespread smuggling of people and drugs proliferate at every U.S. port of entry, the border with Canada, and, most seriously, at the border with Mexico. The need for reform is clear when we look at those who attempt to enforce our current laws, and those whom they seek to keep out, in the following sections.

The Border Patrol

The agency entrusted with assuring that our borders are open to those whom our immigration laws admit and closed to those whom they prohibit is the Immigration and Naturalization Service, the INS. The Border Patrol is its division charged with insuring the security of our borders. Sorting out citizens from uninvited visitors is probably the most difficult and controversy-plagued task of the INS, but those who try to enter our country illegally are only a fraction of the hundreds of millions of people the INS deals with each year. Indeed, as John M. Crewdson, author of *The Tarnished Door*, reported in 1980, in a special series of investigative articles in the *New York Times*, "Each year the service comes into contact with, and has substantial control over the destinies of more human beings than any government agency in the free world."

In one recent year officers of the INS inspected some 270 million people's visas, passports, citizenship papers, birth certificates, nonresident-alien's border-crossing identification cards, cards of identity and registration, work permits (so-called green cards), Social

Security cards, driver's licenses, even baptism certificates. According to Crewdson, these people were "not just the one million individuals arrested for illegal entry by the Border Patrol and the hundreds of thousands of aliens seeking legal entry, but also the many millions of foreign and American citizens who regularly cross the Mexican and Canadian borders and arrive from overseas to shop, work, sightsee, or visit friends." The INS is entrusted with the awesome responsibility of protecting the rights of present and would-be U.S. citizens and maintaining the security of our borders, while at the same time dealing fairly and lawfully with citizens of the rest of the world in our country.

The U.S./Mexico Border

Only about four hundred to five hundred or so Border Patrol agents are on duty at any time throughout the country. Most of these agents work across the border from the Mexican cities of Tijuana and Juarez, in California and Texas. In Los Angeles, where it is estimated that one resident in ten is an illegal alien, the Border Patrol are nearly at a loss to deal with the situation. The overworked and underpaid INS workers cannot keep out the steady stream of aliens from Mexico and those from the Caribbean and Central and South America who attempt to enter the United States at the Mexican border.

The economic situation in their country and the relatively easy access to the United States at the border seem to encourage rather than discourage Mexicans in particular to attempt illegal entry to the United States. More than 50 percent of Mexico's work force have no jobs, or inadequate ones. This situation is bound to get worse, since Mexico's population is predicted to double by the end of the century. Most of the illegal aliens come from the poor countryside, where the economy is at its worst. Those who have petitioned to enter the United States legally number about one million. Many on the list may be forced to wait ten years to get a visa. Yet the temptation for some is too strong: for only a few hundred dollars a prospective alien can arrange to be smuggled into the United States in a matter of a few days.

The two busiest areas of the U.S./Mexico border are at Chula Vista, California, south of San Diego, and El Paso, Texas. It is easier for would-be immigrants to cross in urban areas like El Paso, where one side of the border is an American city, and the other side the Mexican city of Juarez. Those who cross the line splitting Juarez from El Paso attempt to mingle unnoticed among Mexicans who cross the border legally to work (three hundred thousand have credentials that permit them to pass each day) and Mexican Americans who are U.S. citizens. In certain outskirts of the city, those who seek illegal entry find that after crossing the river, making it across the first fifty yards in from the border without being detected by the Border Patrol is the most difficult part of their entry into the country. Then blending in with the rest of the populace becomes their next challenge.

One recent apprehension tells the story of many that take place in and near El Paso. A Border Patrol helicopter pilot sighted and then tracked a Mexican man and two women, following them into a housing development where they tried to hide. The pilot flushed them out, pinning them in a cul-de-sac. Next a van pulled up and two patrolmen jumped out to arrest the Mexicans. The dramatic chase seemed not to excite the patrolmen or even shake the apprehended aliens. Each knew this drama would occur again, even with the same participants.

Once an alien has made it across the border or through a port into the United States, the likelihood that he or she will escape detection is great. Even if they are detected, aliens frequently elude the law and remain in the United States. This is possible since there are more aliens than funds. As it is, the government spends over a million dollars each year to send aliens back to distant countries; the expense of transporting an alien home to Hong Kong, for example, can be a thousand dollars or more. As a result, some aliens when detected in the United States are simply given a letter directing them to return to their own countries. Many then move or hide and change identities to avoid having to leave. Mexicans who are found living here illegally are transported merely one mile back across the border, where they generally wait until the coast is clear and make plans to reenter the United States, perhaps even as soon as a few hours later.

Corruption in the INS

Instances of corruption in the INS were widely reported during the 1970s and early 1980s. As the influx of immigrants grew, so did the stories of illegal acts by the very agency set up to enforce the law.

The story of Joe Seung Chiu, a Chinese teenager, is but one example of corruption in the INS. Mr. Chiu jumped ship in New York harbor in the early 1970s. Like many other illegal aliens living in the United States, he took a job and nervously waited for "the Immigration" to track him down. His job as a cook in a Chinese restaurant was comfortable, and he was able to save some money. But his worries began to nag at him, and he decided he would like to become "legal." The list of Chinese from Hong Kong and Taiwan waiting for visas from the State Department as legal immigrants was very long, and Mr. Chiu was tired of looking over his shoulder for the INS. He sought a faster way than the legal route. Withdrawing fifteen thousand dollars from his savings, he gave it to an acquaintance in exchange for a "green card," the work permit issued to permanent resident aliens by the INS.

With his new credential, Mr. Chiu could work and live in the United States without fear of deportation. Everything was fine until the man who had issued Mr. Chiu's card and those of at least thirty-six other aliens was arrested by the FBI. This man was William V. Tubbs, a supervisory immigration inspector at the San Francisco International Airport and the subject of one of the few cases of INS corruption that has reached the courtroom. Mr. Chiu was one of those who testified against the fifty-two-year-old INS veteran. The government charged Mr. Tubbs with violating immigration law. His prosecutors accused him of issuing the thirty-seven or more green cards, selling them through intermediaries for as much as twenty thousand dollars each. Tubbs denied the charges, but he was convicted of the crime.

Although only a few of the instances of alleged corruption have been made public, those that have indicate the extent of the problem. The last three months of 1980 give a picture of widespread corruption, to a degree unmatched by any other federal law enforcement agency. In October of that year Representative Preyer, a Democrat who headed the House Government Operations Committee, revealed that a number of INS employees were being investigated for "selling or altering immigration documents." In November an El Paso Border Patrol agent was under arrest for offering to sell an INS Form I-186, the valuable but temporary border-crossing permit, for two thousand dollars. And in December 1980 the INS made public the fact that six employees of its New York City office had taken bribes to "tamper with" official INS records and had been convicted.

The corruption in the INS is not limited to taking bribes. Those interviewed in the investigation gave reports of ranchers and other businessmen being in effect exempted from having to observe the immigration laws, extortion of sexual relations in exchange for admission to the United States, and a general laxity in doing the job of apprehending illegal aliens at the border. And it has been further charged that the INS, when confronted with instances of corruption, frequently ignores them or covers them up.

In the 1970s the Justice Department conducted Operation Cleansweep, an inquiry into INS corruption. For nearly three years they gathered allegations and evidence showing that more than 150 past and present INS employees had participated in smuggling both illegal aliens and narcotics into this country, taken kickbacks from government contractors, committed perjury and fraud, obstructed justice, physically abused aliens, and even murdered. Alan M. Murray, one of the Cleansweep investigators, said, "The only crime we didn't find was bank robbery."

Pervasive Violence

In March 1980 a border patrolman shot and killed one young Mexican man and wounded another when they tried to run across the border back toward Mexico, a distance of fifty feet. The patrolman was not charged. The year before, another agent shot an alien twice in the back. But shootings are by no means the only violence along the border. Brutality is the modus operandi of many agents. Those who defend the Border Patrol's tactics say that they face mighty volleys of rocks and bottles and occasionally gunfire from the Mexican side of the border. But those who do engage in rock throwing are mainly young thugs from Tijuana who get kicks from harassing the Border Patrol, not the serious crossers who simply wish to get across with no trouble. A senior immigration official quoted by the *New York Times* in its investigative reports in 1980 gave a good picture of the serious crossers: "These are law-abiding people. We have had cases where a border patrolman who has caught more people than he can move puts one of the aliens in charge of 50. He goes and calls for a bus and when he gets back they're sitting there. They are a very fatalistic people. They all know the old saying, 'Esta es mi vida desgraciada,' 'This is my hard-luck life.' "

The Justice Department officials investigating cases of brutality say there is not enough money or personnel to prosecute all the complaints against the Border Patrol. Many officials suggest that the corruption and violence in the Border Patrol result from the type of person willing to undertake the job, one who is generally unprepared to handle its demands. The salary is low, and the demands of the job are enormous. Overtime pay can raise a patrolman's wages significantly, but by federal standards their starting salary of thirteen thousand dollars is not high. Bribes often add a sort of illegal "bonus."

Border Patrol agents work mostly at night, with little supervision. The job is sometimes dangerous, often difficult and frustrating to those who take it seriously. Many agents feel they are charged with enforcing an immigration policy that cannot be enforced in the ways currently practiced. Almost everyone on both sides of the issue agrees that more must be done to protect illegal aliens from the brutality at the border and also eliminate conditions that make the Border Patrol's job one that encourages corruption and violence. This is the chief reason why the Simpson-Mazzoli bill's proposed use of employer sanctions and guest-worker programs as well as amnesty for those already here are the least controversial measures for reform.

While the debate over how to gain control of our borders continues in Congress and in public forums and private homes throughout the country, the harsh reality of the illegal immigrants' lives remains unimproved. The following stories of two undocumented workers, Felipe Sánchez and Anna Hernández (their names have been changed to protect their identities), show some of the typical situations these aliens encounter in attempting to enter the United States and then in living and working here.

Mr. Sánchez, a Salvadoran, entered illegally by way of Mexico, while Ms. Hernández, a Dominican, came in at the port of New York. Millions of others with similar stories have come here—from Mexico, Colombia, Ecuador, Costa Rica, Jamaica, Haiti, and virtually every other nation in the Caribbean basin and Central and South America. All have sought the "American dream," but to some the situation would appear to be more of a nightmare full of danger and deprivation.

Felipe Sánchez, Undocumented Worker from El Salvador

"I don't know how long I can be here. I'm always waiting to be caught." That is how Felipe Sánchez, a twenty-six-year-old lamp welder in a small factory in Long Island City, New York, describes his life in the United States. Although his life here is bleak and sometimes dangerous, his past in El Salvador was even less hopeful. He had been trained as a welder in a special program and had been working at his job since he was fourteen, but the economic and political situation in his country blocked advancement. His salary of nearly one hundred dollars a month, considered good in El Salvador, could hardly support himself and his dependent sister. A young man, he felt his life was over unless he left El Salvador. As he sadly remembers, "Our government does not help its poor people. We have no land, no rights. Only the rich run the country. They have everything, the poor nothing."

Felipe got together with some of his family to discuss what he should do. "They said, 'Go to the United States. That way you can work for yourself and send some money home for your sister too.' " They had all heard reports of a better life in North America. "In my town," Felipe said, "people would tell stories about the good life in the United States." Reports of others from his factory who had left the country for jobs in New York's light manufacturing and garment industries, which rely heavily on undocumented workers from Latin America, encouraged Felipe to take all the money he had and try to get to America's largest city—port of entry for its first wave of immigrants and now home to at least 850,000 deportable aliens.

A Well-Traveled Route

Without a visa permitting legal immigration, Felipe had the most difficult task ahead of him—getting into the United States without detection. After that, he had heard, getting a job would be fairly easy. The well-traveled route he took was north by air to Mexico City on a tourist pass, then overland, hitching a ride on a truck to Mexico's border with California. Mexican police stopped him en route to Tijuana, identifying him as a foreigner. They threatened him with arrest unless he paid them one hundred dollars, essentially a bribe, to continue. He gave them the money and finally made it to Tijuana, where he paid a taxi driver to transport him to the border. He hoped he would be able to find a "coyote" (smuggler) there to take him across to California. But the driver was not new to this game; he alerted the Mexican border guards to Felipe's unlawful presence by flashing his car lights. These guards then demanded an additional "fine." For $150, presumably shared by the taxi driver, they permitted Felipe to pass and even helped him locate a coyote, who escorted Felipe through the huge drainage tunnels that line the border.

Held Hostage

On the other side at last, Felipe was not yet free. The coyote placed him in the trunk of a car, in which he was taken to Los Angeles. There the coyote and his accomplice, the driver of the car, held Felipe hostage in an old house in a Hispanic neighborhood. They threatened to turn him over to INS officials unless he paid another four hundred dollars. Felipe was held for over two weeks before relatives sent him the money. But the coyote was still not satisfied. He demanded more money. Finally he let Felipe go when Felipe discovered the coyote too was undocumented, or illegal, and at risk of being identified and deported.

Felipe had just enough money left (hidden from the coyote) for the long bus ride to New York. He was excited and anxious all the way across the country, eager to begin his new life and still fearful of being caught. Finally he got to New York, tired and penniless. He had dreamed of arriving in a different way—greeted by some of his countrymen and going out dancing to celebrate. Reality was beginning to change his expectations.

Like many other undocumented aliens, Felipe had little idea of what life in the United States would really be like. He was very clear about what prompted him to leave his country, but his concept of his future was vague, based more on wishful thinking than on solid information. He thought that perhaps he could save enough money to return to his country and start a business or develop additional skills for a new career. When he quickly got a job in a Queens lamp factory that paid in one week what it took a month to make in El Salvador, his hopes were renewed. But he soon learned that the high cost of living in New York cut his profits drastically, even though he kept his expenses to a minimum by living near the factory in a Jackson Heights apartment with four other young men from El Salvador.

Diversity Accepted

This mixed neighborhood serves many immigrants—both legal and illegal, new and old. Jewish delis, Italian cheese stores, Chinese restaurants, Korean fruit stands, and Hispanic *bodegas* (grocery stores) represent a succession of immigrants who moved there in stages. The fact that it is a multilingual area also encourages aliens to seek living quarters there. Felipe had little need to learn English at first because of the many Spanish-speaking residents. And those with expired tourist visas and no green cards could blend in easily with the legal immigrants and refugees.

Trabajo Chiquito

Felipe's search for a job brought success—of a kind—in just one day. He borrowed a Social Security card from a family friend, circumventing the black market and avoiding paying an exorbitant price. The man in the lamp factory who hired him simply glanced at the card, not even checking to see whose name it bore. He gave Felipe a job welding lamp parts, the sort of light manufacturing job that, along with jobs in assembly and shipping as well as repair and cleaning, is typical of the work for which undocumented workers and unskilled or non-English-speaking immigrants are frequently limited to doing. One such worker called them *trabajo chiquito*, "little jobs."

Felipe also followed the pattern set by many other undocumented aliens: he seized this job without bargaining over wages or working conditions. Even though he was a skilled welder, he was largely ignorant of how to conduct himself in the labor market. He felt he was in no position to negotiate, especially with his poor command of English, for fear of being turned down and refused the job. When asked whether he thought his employer specifically sought out illegal workers for *trabajo chiquito*, Felipe said, "No. But it works out that they end up using us and are happy. They would take anyone who would do the job. People in the U.S. don't want these jobs. They're for people like us. We have to do anything that comes along to stay alive."

Staying alive in some of the work places of *trabajo chiquito* is frequently no easy task. The working conditions at Felipe's factory were similar to others employing undocumented workers—cold in winter, sweltering in summer, dusty and dark, even dangerous. At first Felipe worked at a kind of kiln, and often his hands were nearly burned as he removed metal from the heat. He knew of others who spent their days breathing the heavy industrial dust from cut fabric until at night their noses would bleed from the irritation. He had heard too the story of the little girl who fell six stories to her death in a open, unmarked elevator shaft in a factory building while her father worked nearby. The elevator had three citations for safety violations at the time. Such sweatshop conditions are not unusual in these industries. They allow small, low-budget contractors to bring down production costs and undercut union shops paying higher wages. Sweatshops generally do not pay overtime or benefits to the workers or payments to the government for unemployment insurance or other taxes. Their proprietors may capitalize on the vulnerability of undocumented workers like Felipe.

At first Felipe worked seven days a week, nine hours a day. The overtime hours were not always at the demand of the boss. Felipe needed to make more money to send back to his sister. The high cost of living in New York ate away at his salary. After a year, he finally asked for—and got—a raise of ten dollars a week.

His work is everything to him. "I go from home to work, work to home. I am not free to do anything but work. Sometimes even there I am afraid the immigration will come to get me. Then what would I do?" In addition to his fear of a *denuncia*, an anonymous telephone call to the INS by a jealous co-worker or angry boss informing on an undocumented worker, Felipe is afraid of getting sick and not being able to work. He goes to an herb seller to buy teas and ointments made of herbs found in Central and South America. He prays that his health will continue to be good. And he is thinking about trying to find a union job that would pay for medical care and provide insurance.

Arranged Marriages

Felipe has also been thinking about marriage. If he married an American citizen or legal resident, he would become eligible for a permanent visa and a green card that would give him status as a legal immigrant. Today the marriage market in New York and other immigrant centers is a booming business. Arranged marriages, called *arreglos*, cost from six hundred to fifteen hundred dollars, plus perhaps another fifteen hundred dollars or so in lawyer's fees. The INS has become justly suspicious of these *arreglos*; they have been known to visit the married couple's address unannounced to check that both sleep there, as well as conduct intimate interviews with each member of the couple to verify their true relationship. Despite these obstacles, Felipe, perhaps naively, sees an *arreglo* as one way out of his trap. For now, however, he will continue to spend nearly all his time at work, the one place he feels most secure. As he says, "I am married to my work, and my fear."

Anna Hernández, Undocumented Worker from Dominican Republic

Anna Hernández is one of the estimated 250,000 Dominicans living in New York City. Like about half of her countrymen and women in the city, she is an illegal alien, an undocumented factory worker in New York's garment industry, long the work place of immigrants—first Jewish and other primarily Eastern Europeans, now Asians, Latin Americans, and Caribbeans.

Like most of the other Dominicans living and working illegally in New York, Anna, who was twenty-four when she left home for the United States four years ago, is young and skilled.

Although her story is similar to that of many other undocumented women garment workers, it belies the stereotypical image of illegal aliens that many hold. She came not from the impoverished countryside but from the capital of the Dominican Republic. Not the inexperienced, illiterate *bracero,* a male with no education and only obsolete farming skills, Anna is literate, had studied in a vocational business school after completing the eleventh grade, and had three years' experience as a seamstress. Her departure from her country means a loss of resources for her native land. Considering her assets, why would she and those like her choose to leave?

Although she had studied secretarial skills for three months, hoping to land a good job, she ended up sewing underwear in a large factory. Two hundred other women like her worked there for long hours and low pay. Anna became an excellent skilled seamstress, but she knew she had no future at the factory. "The factory owners prefer young girls. I had worked there from age 21 to 24. I wanted a better life." She sought the only way out—migration.

A Tourist Visa

Anna had heard from her cousin Pedro, who was working as a fabric cutter in New York, that she would be able to find work easily in New York's garment center. She began to look for a way to obtain a tourist visa, ostensibly to visit Pedro for only a few months and not to work. This family network and use of a visitor's visa are frequent means of passage. After the few months' time in the United States granted by the visa have elapsed, most aliens remain in the country and become "illegal." Although the most accessible way to enter the United States, tourist visas can be difficult to obtain. A visitor must substantiate his or her intention to return to the home country, generally by showing proof of a sizable bank account, title to a home and car, and a return-trip ticket.

The one-way ticket from the Dominican Republic to New York was less than two hundred dollars, but Anna was forced to go into greater debt to her family to get a visa. She had two options—both costly. She could have done what others before her had done and asked her relatives to put up their homes for collateral on a loan for a bank account large enough to secure the visa she needed and to prove, falsely, intent to return. But she was afraid: "If I was caught and deported, I knew I would not be able to pay off the loan. My family would lose their home." But she chose the second option, like those she had heard about who were able to purchase false papers and "rent" a bank account through the black market.

Established black marketeers hawked their services each morning openly on the long lines for visa applications outside the consul's office. Anna paid one of these extortionists eight hundred dollars, which she had borrowed from her aunt and uncle, for a resident card and passport, neither of which was in her name. She anxiously purchased her airline ticket with money Pedro had sent her and left the next morning, full of expectations of a new life. When she arrived at New York's Kennedy Airport, Anna was met by an accomplice of the man who had sold her the papers she used to pass through immigration and customs checks. She returned to him the documents, as agreed when she paid for their use. Undoubtedly many others had entered and would again enter the United States using the very same passport and resident card.

Pedro and his wife also met Anna at the airport. Together they took her by bus to her new home, a two-room apartment in a tenement building on Ninth Avenue, in Manhattan's Chelsea, a heterogeneous neighborhood of wealthy townhouse owners, impoverished black and Hispanic tenement dwellers, and young middle-class professionals living in high-priced apartments. The apartment in which Anna began her life in the United States housed three other Dominican women, all garment workers. Down the hall Pedro, his wife, Elena, and their three children lived in a similar apartment.

Few Questions from Employers

Anna knew the first thing she had to do was find a job. She had to pay back her family for the money she had borrowed to get to the United States, and she knew they expected her to help support her younger sisters and brothers as soon as she could.

Pedro gave thirty dollars to one of the other women in Anna's apartment so that Anna could use her Social Security card to find work. He knew that with her sewing experience she would have little trouble getting a job. In the garment industry few employers asked for an applicant to show a *tarjeta,* the valuable green card, and most would not look carefully at a Social Security card. (A 1974 regulation restricted Social Security cards to U.S. citizens and legal residents, and consequently these cards became expensive commodities on the black market.)

Anna's contacts through Pedro and her new network of aliens from her country led her to a job in the first place she looked—a small sportswear factory, a nonunion "sweatshop" in the South Bronx, about a forty-five minute subway ride from her new home.

Anna quickly became used to the life of an undocumented worker. She earned $120 a week on her first job, much more than in her homeland. But her expenses were high. She paid seventy dollars a month in rent, and that plus transportation, food, and payments on her loans from her family took everything she earned.

Poor Working Conditions

At first Anna was pleased with her salary. She was earning as much in one week as she would have earned in six weeks at home. Like others who owed hundreds, and in some cases thousands, of dollars to those who helped finance their trips, Anna was inclined to take her pay and put up with the poor working conditions and inequities of the job. Anna and the women who worked with her were paid by the personal check of the sweatshop owner, who deducted disability, social security, and taxes but most likely did not report them to the government. Anna cashed her check in a rundown check-cashing storefront in her neighborhood. She could not, however, file for benefits or collect overpaid taxes since her presence would be detected. As Anna quickly found out, "The state gets the benefits, not us. We have no rights."

One evening as she left the check-cashing store after cashing her week's paycheck, Anna was accosted by two teenage thugs who stole her purse after throwing her to the ground. She broke her arm in the fall, requiring her to pay two hundred dollars for emergency room treatment at a city hospital and to spend a week home from work without pay. The disability payments deducted from her check each week could have covered her expenses and time off, but she could not collect anything for fear of detection.

Soon after she was able to return to work, Anna was laid off. The garment business has occasional slack periods, and undocumented workers are the first to be laid off at such times. Desperately worried that she would not be able to pay her bills and would sink further into debt to her family, Anna took the first job she heard about, in another small sweatshop, this time in Brooklyn. Here she was paid $110 in cash, entirely "off the books," which was more than her take-home pay on the previous job but the money came at a high cost. The cost was speed. Anna was exploited because the forelady in the shop knew she was desperate for money and afraid of being detected by immigration officers as an undocumented worker. The fact that Anna was laid off and yet could not collect unemployment compensation tipped off the forelady to her plight and her undocumented, illegal status. As a result, she pushed Anna to do more work than anyone else. Anna remembers: "She sent me all the work others had done wrong to fix. She piled my machine high with work. I had to stay until the work was done, no matter how late it was. I wasn't permitted to say a word."

Anna was afraid to say anything for fear that she would be caught. Once her boss waited for her outside the bathroom; when she came out he told her he just had had a visit from the INS, looking for illegal workers. Later other workers told her he was lying, to intimidate her. She felt as if she was always looking over her shoulder, expecting to be caught. Her nervousness was aggravated by the INS practice of selecting sites to raid in response to *denuncias* by informants. Even after eight months in this job, Anna feared that her harsh forelady would betray her to the INS.

One of Anna's roommates had found work in a union shop. Anna knew her skills were good enough to work there too. She took her chances. The lure of a fair wage and better working conditions drew her to the union, in this case the International Ladies Garment Workers Union (ILGWU), which is one of the two unions in the New York apparel industry. At first she was afraid that a union job would require a green card, but others had told her that wasn't true. She applied for work in the same blouse factory as her roommate and got a job paying the then union minimum of $3.80 an hour, with benefits, overtime pay, and better working conditions. Today she's still at that same factory, in a better job. She has paid back her family and now regularly sends them fifty dollars a month for her brothers' and sisters' education.

Anna's life is more secure now that she has a better job, but she still fears the INS, who have been known to resort to surprise raids on work places and homes suspected of employing and housing illegal aliens. Anna has heard of immigrants being caught this way, arrested, and detained in an INS facility in Brooklyn known to be worse than any jail. "I can't even be myself," she says. "I'm always on guard, watching, afraid of letting anyone know my story, my problem."

Cannot Return

One of the most frustrating and painful conditions of Anna's status has been her inability ever to go back to her country. To do so would mean she would never be able to return to the United States. Last year Anna's father was hospitalized with a severe stroke that threatened his life. The agony of knowing he would die soon and she would not be able to see him again was one of the hardest things for Anna to bear. "I knew if I went to see him, I could not get back in. I had dreams, terrible dreams. He is dead now. I could not even see him buried." Recently Anna's younger sister wrote to her saying she wanted to come to the United States too and work as Anna had done. Anna prayed all night after receiving the letter. She asked, "God, what shall I tell my sister?"

The Future

Anna's dilemma about what advice to give her younger sister may find its solution when Congress resolves the current differences among its members in the House and Senate over immigration reform. It has been more than two years since the Speaker of the House of Representatives, Thomas P. O'Neill, Jr., received a telegram signed by former presidents Jimmy Carter and Gerald Ford and other political, business, and labor leaders on the President's Select Committee appointed to study our immigration policies. The telegram urged Speaker O'Neill to bring the controversial Simpson-Mazzoli bill before the House.

> Dear Mr. Speaker: America's immigration policies are in a shambles. . . . We realize that this issue is complex and difficult; the amendments must be debated on the House floor; and that other national priorities compete for the attention of the House. This problem is too serious for further delay. . . . The American people are impatient. The failure to bring this bill up will arouse cynicism about the will of the House to face tough issues, and dangerous

> feelings of animosity toward all immigration—legal and illegal alike. We urge you to bring this bill before the House, now.

A version of the bill was passed by the Senate in 1982, and finally, after extended political maneuvering by Democrats and Republicans alike, especially those with large Hispanic constituencies, the House passed its own version in the summer of 1984. The necessary conferencing between the Senate and the House to resolve differences and come to a compromise over certain provisions of the bill was postponed until after the presidential nominating campaigns of both parties, where it ran into a political quagmire. Candidates of both parties rejected it, clearly in deference to Hispanic leaders, who conducted a vigorous campaign against it.

Despite the problems it encountered in gaining acceptance, the Simpson-Mazzoli bill basically attempts to gain greater control of our borders and to protect all members of our society—those who have been born here and those who are the new immigrants, legal and illegal alike. Most people agree with its intentions and its reforms. But it will take time and increased enforcement to reform our out-of-date system, even with Simpson-Mazzoli. The bill is not a cure-all, but it attempts to reduce the inequities and impose necessary restrictions.

The controversy over Simpson-Mazzoli and how to keep our doors open while at the same time reform inequities or injustices and protect all who seek to live and work here will continue as long as Americans struggle to uphold our heritage of welcome to the world's citizens in the face of modern political and social realities. Our open doors have seen a new kind of immigrant pass through them in the past twenty years. Most who have come since we last amended our laws have been Hispanic and Asian. While once we welcomed the Germans, Irish, and

Italians, for example, today we have opened our doors to the Mexicans, Cubans, Koreans, Vietnamese, and others of Hispanic and Asian nationalities. Many have come as legal immigrants after frequently enduring long waits for official entry, or as refugees from war-torn or politically unstable nations. But at least an equal number have come illegally—buying forged documents on the black market to enter, overstaying the terms of legal visas, or smuggling themselves across the border.

How to protect our laws, our language, our jobs, our economy, our natural resources—these are some of the concerns frequently expressed during the debate over immigration reform. These concerns are in a delicate balance with our welcome to the new immigrants. No one knows exactly what effect immigration will have in the last part of the century or how best to secure the rights of both present and future U.S. citizens. But few would maintain that the effort is not worth undertaking.

Our nation's open arms to the world have become one of our most cherished symbols. It is in the highest interest of our national identity to do something about the shambles of the current immigration situation. The facelift the once-majestic Statue of Liberty is now receiving must be more than skin deep if we hope to continue to fulfill the promise of the open door and hold high the lamp of liberty to today's new immigrants, and tomorrow's.

FOR FURTHER READING

Cafferty, P. *The Dilemma of American Immigration: Beyond the Golden Door.* San Francisco: Transaction Books, 1983.

Ehrlich, Paul R. *The Golden Door: International Migration, Mexico, and the U.S.* New York: Ballantine, 1979.

Handlin, Oscar. *The Uprooted,* 2d ed. Boston: Little Brown, 1973.

Harper, Elizabeth. *Immigration Laws of the United States,* 3d ed. Indianapolis: Bobbs-Merrill, 1975.

Haskins, James. *The New Americans, Cuban Boat People.* Hillside, NJ: Enslow Publishers, 1982.

Higham, John. *Send These to Me.* New York: Atheneum, 1975.

Knoll, Tricia. *Becoming Americans: Asian Sojourners, Immigrants, and Refugees in the Western United States.* Portland, OR: Coast to Coast Books, 1982.

Kraus, Michael, and Louis L. Synder. *Immigration, the American Mosaic: From Pilgrims to Modern Refugees.* Huntington, N.Y.: Krieger, 1979.

Matthews, Carey, *Strike from Mariel.* Boston: First Commonwealth, 1983.

Philipson, Lorrin, and Rafael Llerena. *Freedom Flights.* New York: Random House, 1980.

IMMIGRATION-RELATED ORGANIZATIONS

American Friends Service Committee
Mexico/U.S. Border Program
1501 Cherry Street
Philadelphia, Pennsylvania 19102
(215) 864-0204

American Immigration Lawyers Association
1000 16th St., N.W.,
Washington, DC 20036
(202) 331-0046

Center for Migration Studies
209 Flagg Place
Staten Island, New York 10304
(212) 351-8800

Centro Para Immigrantes
2314 Cochran
Houston, Texas 77023
(713) 228-0091

Church World Service Immigration
and Refugee Program
475 Riverside Drive
New York, New York 10115
(212) 870-2164

Committee for Fair Immigration Legislation
c/o Center for Immigrants' Rights
2525 Broadway, #8
New York, New York 10025
(212) 759-1424

Farm Worker Defense Committee
c/o Javier Aguirre
804 Decatur Street
Sunnyside, Washington 98944

Federation for American Immigration Reform (FAIR)
2028 P Street, NW
Washington, DC 20036
(202) 785-3474

Indochina Refugee Action Center
1424 16th Street, NW
Washington, DC 20036
(202) 667-7810

League of United Latin American Citizens (LULAC)
400 First Street, NW
Washington, DC 20001
(202) 628-0717

LULAC National Office
400 First Street, NW, #721
Washington, DC 20001
(202) 628-0717

Lutheran Council in the U.S.A.
Department of Immigration and Refugee Services
360 Park Avenue South
New York, New York 10010
(212) 532-6350

Mexican-American Legal Defense and Education Fund (MALDEF)
1701 18th Street, NW
Washington, DC 20005
(202) 393-5111

National Committee Against Repressive Legislation
201 Massachusetts Avenue, NE
Washington, DC 20002
(202) 543-7659

National Council of La Raza
20F I Street, NW
Washington, DC 20006
(202) 293-4680

National Immigration, Refugee, and Citizenship Forum
533 Eighth St., S.E.
Washington, DC 20003
(202) 544-0004

North American Congress on Latin America
151 West 19th Street
New York, New York 10011
(212) 989-8890

Oxfam America
115 Broadway
Boston, Massachusetts 02116
(617) 482-1211

Population Association of America
806 15th Street, NW
Washington, DC 20005
(202) 393-3253

The Population Council
One Dag Hammarskjold Plaza
New York, New York 10017
(212) 644-1300

Population Institute
110 Maryland Avenue, NE
Washington, DC 20002
(202) 544-3300

Population Reference Bureau
1337 Connecticut Avenue, NW
Washington, DC 20036
(202) 785-4664

Population Resource Center
110 Maryland Avenue, NE
Washington, DC 20002
(202) 546-5030

Refugee Action Group
1424 16th Street, NW
Washington, DC 20036
(202) 667-7810

U.S. English
1648 16th Street, NW
Washington, DC 20036
(202) 232-5200

United States Catholic Conference
Migration and Refugee Service
1312 Massachusetts Avenue, NW
Washington, DC 20005
(202) 659-6625

World Population Society
1337 Connecticut Avenue, NW, Suite 200
Washington, DC 20036
(202) 833-2440

INDEX

Afghanistan, 37
Africa, 37
Agriculture, 78
Alabama, 65
American Civil Liberties Union, 82
American Federation of Labor-Congress of Industrial Organizations (AFL-CIO), 82
Amnesty, 82–84
Amnesty International, 67
Arizona, 15
Arkansas, 40, 62, 66
Arranged marriages, 97–98
Asian immigrants, 3, 6, 7, 8, 9, 15, 18–26, 39-56. *See also specific nationalities*
Assimilation process, 10
Asylum, 41, 68, 72
Auto industry, 78

Ballots, bilingual, 30
Bilingual Education Act, 30
Bilingualism, 26, 29–33
Blacks, 79
Boat people, 41–42
Border Patrol, 79, 85–88, 89, 90–91
Bribes, 88–90, 93
British immigrants, 9
Bronx, New York, 24, 25
Brooklyn, New York, 7, 24, 25

California, 10, 11, 15, 16, 18, 20-22, 40, 48, 78, 86, 87
Cambodian immigrants, 24, 40–41
Canada, 6, 30–31, 85, 86
Caribbean immigrants, 6, 7, 9, 15, 38, 66, 70–72, 78. *See also specific nationalities*
Carter, Jimmy, 8, 61, 62, 84, 104
Castro, Fidel, 10, 17, 59–61, 63, 64, 65, 71
Catholicism, 15
Catholic Relief Services, 46
Central America, 15, 16, 66
Chavez, Cesar, 23
Chicago, Illinois, 11

Chinese immigrants, 6, 19, 24, 25, 30, 42, 88–89
Chiu, Joe Seung, 88–89
Chu, Anthony, 19
Chula Vista, California, 87
Church groups, 68–69
Colorado, 11, 15, 19
Communism, 38, 40, 42, 43, 44
Congress, 4, 5, 33, 37, 81, 91, 104–105
Constitution, 22
Corruption, INS, 88–90
Council of Jewish Federation, 73
Coyote, 93, 94
Crewdson, John M., 85, 86
Crime, 64–65, 66, 88–90, 93–94. *See also* Illegal aliens
Cuban immigrants, 7, 8, 10, 11, 15, 17–18, 37, 59–66, 71
Cuban Patriotic Junta, 63
Cultural identity, 31–32, 52, 53

Darbouze, Rollin, 70, 71
Del Rio, Texas, 10
Denver, Colorado, 11
Deportation, 77, 80, 81, 88, 89
Dominican immigrants, 6, 98–104
Dutch immigrants, 9
Duvalier, Jean-Claude, 70, 71, 72

Eastern Europe, 9, 37
Economic issues, 16, 33, 38, 65, 71, 77–79, 81–85, 86, 92
Education, 33, 34, 65; bilingual, 29–33
Eglin Air Force Base, Florida, 61–62, 66
El Paso, Texas, 87, 89
El Salvadoran immigrants, 38, 66–70, 92–98
Emigrant, defined, 6
Employer sanctions, 81–82, 91
Employment, 4, 10, 11, 15, 65, 73; and illegal aliens, 77–79, 81–85, 95–104
Ethnic differences, 9–10
European immigrants, 6, 7, 9

Family relationships, 6, 10
Ferre, Maurice, 57
Filipino immigrants, 7, 19, 23–24, 29
First asylum, 41

Fisherfolk, Vietnamese, 51–56
Florida, 3, 10, 11, 15, 17, 40, 51–56, 59–66
Ford, Gerald, 84, 104
Fort Chaffee, Arkansas, 40, 62, 66
Fort Indiantown Gap, Pennsylvania, 66
Fort McCoy, Wisconsin, 66
French immigrants, 9

Gangplank mentality, 64
Garment industry, 78, 98, 99, 102, 103
Gaudie, Cecil, 66
Gelber, Seymour, 66
Green card, 85, 88, 89, 101
Guest workers, 84–85, 91
Gulf Coast, 51–56

Haitian immigrants, 7, 8, 10, 12, 38, 70–72
Hawaii, 7
Hayakawa, S.I., 32–33
Hebrew Immigrants Aid Society, 73
Hesburgh, Theodore, 84
Hispanics, 9, 15–18, 30–33, 59–66; illegal aliens, 81–88, 92–104. *See also specific nationalities*
Hmong refugees, 7, 41, 42–48
Holtzman, Elizabeth, 60
Hong Kong, 25, 88
House of Representatives, 81, 104, 105
House Subcommittee on Immigration, Refugees, and International Law, 60
Housing, 65
Hudson County, New Jersey, 17

Illegal aliens, 4, 17, 74, 77–104; defined, 8–9; and employment, 77–79, 81–85, 95–104
Illinois, 11
Immigrant, defined, 6
Immigrant personality, 34
Immigration and Nationality Act, 6–7, 9, 37
Immigration and Naturalization Service (INS), 9, 62, 64, 68, 77, 85, 86, 97, 102–103; corruption in, 88–90
Immigration policy, 4–5, 17, 19, 78, 79–80; national origins system, 6–7; 1965 Immigration and Nationality Act Amendments, 6–7, 9; Refugee Act of 1980, 9,

Immigration policy *(continued)* 37–39, 73; Simpson-Mazzoli bill, 4, 80–85, 91, 104–105
Indochinese immigrants, 8, 37, 39–56
Interagency Task Force on Immigration, 78
International Ladies Garment Workers Union (ILGWU), 103
Irish immigrants, 9
Italian immigrants, 9

Jamaica, 6
Japanese immigrants, 19, 24
Jews, 9; Soviet refugees, 72–74
Jordan, Barbara, 84
Juarez, 86, 87
Justice Department, 90, 91

Kampuchean immigrants. *See* Cambodian immigrants
Khmer, 41
Korean immigrants, 6, 7, 11, 19–23, 24, 25
Korean War, 20

Language, 10, 16, 26, 29–33, 95
Laotian immigrants, 7, 12, 24, 40, 41, 42–48
Laredo, Texas, 10
Latin America, 6, 7, 9, 16, 38
Lau v. Nichols, 29–30
Lazarus, Emma, 1
Legal immigrant, defined, 8
Los Angeles, California, 10, 16, 18, 20–22, 94
Louisiana, 51, 55
Lutheran Immigration and Refugee Service, 66

Marcos, Ferdinand, 23
Mariel boatlift, 17–18, 59–66, 71
Marriages, arranged, 97–98
Marshall, Ray, 79
Mazzoli, Romano, 70, 80
Mexican border, 85, 86–88, 90
Mexican immigrants, 3, 6, 7, 9, 10, 15, 16, 17, 29, 77, 78, 79, 84, 86–88, 90
Miami, Florida, 10, 11, 17, 18, 59–66
Miami International Rescue Committee, 66
Mien, 41
Migration Today, 32
Mississippi, 7

Murray, Alan M., 90

National identity card, 82
National origins system, 6–7
New Jersey, 7, 17–18
New Mexico, 15
Newsweek, 85
New York, 7, 18, 24–25, 89, 93, 94–100
New York Association for New Americans, 73
New York Times, 5, 85, 90

O'Neill, Thomas P., Jr., 104
Operation Cleansweep, 90
Operation Wetback, 83
Oregon, 67, 68

Passport, 100
Pathet Lao, 43, 44
Pennsylvania, 40, 66
Personality, immigrant, 34
Philby, Kim, 59
Philippines. *See* Filipino immigrants
Policy, immigration. *See* Immigration policy
Political issues, 4–5, 16, 34, 38, 64, 67, 70, 71, 72, 77, 81, 92
Providence, Rhode Island, 7

Queens, New York, 24, 25

Reagan, Ronald, 67, 68, 78, 81
Refugee(s), 15, 17–18, 34, 35–74; camps, 40, 62, 66; Cuban, 59–66; defined, 8; El Salvadoran, 66–70; Haitian, 70–72; Indochinese, 39–56; Soviet Jewish, 72–74; status, 68, 70
Refugee Act of 1980, 9, 37–39, 73
Religion, 9, 68–69
Resettlement agencies, 46, 52, 55
Resident card, 100
Restaurant work, 78
Rhode Island, 7
Roosevelt, Theodore, 27

San Antonio, Texas, 7
San Francisco, California, 11, 18, 45
Sarmiento, Jesus, 66
Seattle, Washington, 7, 67, 68–69
Second asylum, 41
Select Committee on Immigration and Refugee Policy, 84, 104

Senate, 4, 81, 105
Senate Subcommittee on Immigration and Refugee Policy, 39
Sequoia, 61
Service industry, 78
Sexual practices, 10
Simpson, Alan, 39, 80
Simpson-Mazzoli bill, 4, 80–85, 91, 104–105
Slavs, 9
Smith, William French, 80
Social behaviors, 6, 10
Social Security card, 95, 100, 101
Society, American, changes in, 9–10
South America, 15, 16, 66
Southeast Asia, 3, 7, 8, 38
Soviet Jewish refugees, 72–74
Soviet Union, 37, 72
Spanish language, 16, 29–33, 64, 95
Statue of Liberty, 3, 106
Suarez, Eduardo, 66
Suburbs, 18, 19
Supreme Court decisions, 29–30
Sweatshops, 96, 101, 102

Taiwan, 6
Temporary-resident status, 83
Texas, 7, 10, 15, 16, 51, 55, 86, 87
Thai immigrants, 24
Thailand, 41, 43, 44
Third World, 6
Tijuana, 86, 90, 93
Tourist visa, 8, 99–100
Tubbs, William V., 89

Undocumented workers. *See* Illegal aliens
Union City, New Jersey, 17
United Farm Workers, 23
United Nations, 37, 38, 40
U.S. citizenship, 22
U.S. Citizenship Petition Oath, 13
U.S. English, 32
U.S./Mexican border, 85, 86–88, 90
Upward mobility, 26, 33–34, 73
Urban growth, 17–18, 64-65

Vietnamese immigrants, 7, 8, 11, 19, 24, 25, 39–48, 51–56
Vietnam War, 8, 39, 41, 42
Viking Starship, 60
Violence, 90–92

Visa, 85, 87; tourist, 8, 99–100
Voting Rights Act, 30

Washington (state), 7, 68–69
White, Theodore, 7
Wisconsin, 45–48, 66
Work styles, 10
World Refugee Survey 1983, 70
World War II, 37

ABOUT THE AUTHORS

Carol Olsen Day is a writer and producer with extensive experience in book publishing and record, film, and theater production. A graduate of George Washington University, she was formerly vice-president and director of publications for Catalyst, the national organization for women and employers. Ms. Day has published articles in a variety of national magazines, and has recently begun to write for television.

Edmund Day graduated from Georgetown University and studied at the Catholic University Graduate School of Speech and Drama. He has worked throughout the country and in New York as a professional actor in more than forty productions and at the same time, he has published articles on a wide range of topics for both adults and young adults.

Carol and Edmund Day live in New York City.